In Praise of *The Works of Mercy*

"Legions of students have heard Father Keenan speak of mercy as our willing entry into the chaos of another person. Now, in the most personal and deeply spiritual of his works, this distinguished moral theologian and priest tells us what mercy means to him. In clear and lyrical style, Father Keenan explores mercy in its biblical roots, the history of the Church, and the contemporary world. The meditations on mercy in light of September 11 and of the Church's sex abuse scandal shine as gems of spiritual autobiography. This is pastorally grounded and compelling spiritual reading that speaks to all of us."—**Paul Crow**~~l~~ ~~……~~ ofessor of religious studies, Santa Clara ~~……~~

"At a time when loud voices s~~e~~ ~~……~~ of Catholic identity is partisan adhe~~i~~ ~~……~~ ve have the voice of Jim Keenan, gen~~t~~ ~~…… back to~~ the real heart of the Catholic faith: ~~……~~ and mercy acted out. Hooray for Father Jim's unequivocal but vulnerable unfolding of the truth that authentic Catholic identity is given to us as we dare to let go of our identity and enter as equals into the pain and confusion of others just as Our Lord entered into ours."—**James Alison**, Catholic theologian, priest, and author of *Faith Beyond Resentment* and *On Being Liked*

"In a world starved for compassion and kindness, Father Keenan brings a sense of expectation and hope for a better future, and invites the reader to fulfill Christ's command to love one another. By describing how the Catholic tradition has honored the command of the Gospel to practice the works of mercy, and also how contemporary Christians continue to fulfill Christ's command to love one another, Father Keenan invites the reader to go and do likewise. Written in a style that is both profound and practical, the book, rich in its use of scripture, is ideal for theological reflection on both the corporal and spiritual works of mercy. In a world filled with suffering, the whole church can benefit from focusing on these words, whether an RCIA group, an adult education class, a small faith sharing group, or a class preparing for confirmation."—**Katarina Schuth, O.S.F.**, Endowed Chair for the Social Scientific Study of Religion, St. Paul Seminary School of Divinity, University of St. Thomas

"There is energy in these pages, the kind of energy that's contagious. I challenge you to read this book and not be affected by it. I predict that you will wind up not only valuing mercy as a virtue and identifying it gratefully in others, but you will also desire a greater share of it as part of your own spiritual DNA. Be prepared for a stunning read and a real gift of light."—**Doris Donnelly**, Ph.D., director of The Cardinal Suenens Center, John Carroll University

The Works of Mercy

A CHURCH BOOK
from the National Pastoral Life Center

The **CHURCH** book series from Sheed & Ward focuses on developing discipleship and leadership, fostering faith formation and moral decision making, and enhancing the Church's worship and social ministry. Titles in the series address clergy, laity, and religious on topics and issues that concern the whole people of God.

Series Editor: Karen Sue Smith

The Works of Mercy

The Heart of Catholicism

James F. Keenan, S.J.

A SHEED & WARD BOOK

ROWMAN & LITTLEFIELD PUBLISHERS, INC.
Lanham • Boulder • New York • Toronto • Oxford

A SHEED & WARD BOOK

ROWMAN & LITTLEFIELD PUBLISHERS, INC.

Published in the United States of America
by Rowman & Littlefield Publishers, Inc.
A wholly owned subsidiary of The Rowman & Littlefield Publishing Group, Inc.
4501 Forbes Boulevard, Suite 200, Lanham, Maryland 20706
www.rowmanlittlefield.com

PO Box 317
Oxford
OX2 9RU, UK

British Library Cataloguing in Publication Information Available

Library of Congress Cataloging-in-Publication Data

Keenan, James F.
  The works of mercy : the heart of Catholicism / James F. Keenan.
    p. cm. — (Church Book Series)
  Includes index.
  ISBN 0-7425-3219-4 (cloth : alk. paper) — ISBN 0-7425-3220-8
(pbk. : alk. paper)
  1. Corporal works of mercy. 2. Spiritual works of mercy.
3. Christian ethics—Catholic authors. I. Title.
BV4647.M4 K44 2004
241'.042—dc22   2004024808

Printed in the United States of America

⊗™ The paper used in this publication meets the minimum requirements of
American National Standard for Information Sciences—Permanence of Paper
for Printed Library Materials, ANSI/NISO Z39.48-1992.

For

AELRED TIMMINS

and

MARGARET A. FARLEY,

Sisters of Mercy

Contents

IV. A Meditation on Priesthood
in Light of the Church's Scandals

V. Mercy and the Eucharistic Liturgy

Acknowledgments

These essays originally appeared in my column in *Church* magazine. For five years I proposed the works of mercy routinely to the readers of *Church,* and each time I came to write the column I became amazed at the richness of our tradition.

As I submitted each column, I had the kind, intelligent, and rigorous editorial mind, heart, and eye of Karen Smith engaging my text. These essays became more enriched by her thoughtful comments. I am indebted to her.

Now I have turned them over to Jeremy Langford at Sheed & Ward knowing that, as always, they will be well prepared by him and Katie Lane for publication. These are people who make the ministry of theological writing a pleasure.

I wrote these at Weston Jesuit School of Theology where a community of students, faculty, staff, and administration frequently taught me in the classroom, at meetings, and in worship the need for mercy in the doing of theology. Now at Boston College I have edited these essays and I encounter yet again God's graciousness especially in the practice of this community's hospitality.

Over the years I learned that God's mercy makes human love possible. I learned this in three particular sets of relationships: those with my family, my friends, and my Jesuit community at 10 Martin Street (aka Zipoli House). God's mercy and their love make my life possible.

Finally, I dedicate this book to two Sisters of Mercy, who have taught me the meaning of mercy. In the spring of 1994 Aelred Timmins welcomed me into her community of the Sisters of Mercy at St.

Catharine's in Edinburgh, Scotland, where I was a fellow at the University. She and her community entered into the chaos of the many homeless looking for sanctuary in that great city. Margaret A. Farley has always been an inspiration for me. Her commitment to her students at Yale Divinity School and to her colleagues in the field of Christian ethics has been for me a model of mercy. By their lives, I have seen mercy at work.

Introduction

$\mathcal{T}$he only principle I really need is mercy," Aelred Timmins once said to me. I was stunned. It seemed so simple yet so complete. In time, her words inspired me to reflect more on mercy in our tradition and in our lives.

On these pages, I try to lay out how mercy has been God's way toward us and our way toward one another. I try to trace these ways through the Scriptures and through the many ways that the church over the centuries has lived mercifully. As I outline these ways, I keep mercy in the forefront, defining it throughout as the willingness to enter the chaos of others to answer them in their need.

I divide the book into three parts. First, the corporal works of mercy, which have provided the focus of ministry to church movements over the centuries: the early monastic communities, the medieval religious orders, the lay associations starting in the twelfth century, the confraternities from the sixteenth century, and those movements of the church in the modern world.

Second, I turn to the spiritual works of mercy, which are more personal in nature than the corporate corporal works of mercy. These can be grouped, as Augustine grouped them, into three categories: reconciliation, the call to be vigilant for the spiritual needs of one's neighbor, and prayer.

Third, because we are called by God's mercy into the church, I look at the effective work of mercy in the prayer of the church, particularly in the Eucharist.

At the end of the first and second parts, I pause to meditate for a moment on mercy in light of September 11, 2001, and in light of the church's scandals.

Mercy Distinguishes Catholic Morality

$\mathcal{I}$s there something about Catholic morality that distinguishes it from the morality of other religious believers? This is a vexing question. It is not a question about superiority. It is simply a question about distinctiveness or uniqueness. It is the question about identity, about what identifies us as Catholic in our moral lives.

The question is vexing because it is difficult to find any one thing that belongs to Catholics *as Catholics*. For instance, we Catholics appreciate the natural law, but, in Romans 1, Saint Paul writes that the natural law is written in everyone's heart; by that law, people can tell right from wrong. Many Catholics believe (rightly) that what is right for Catholics is right for everyone and whatever is wrong for Catholics is equally wrong for everyone.

Others root our morality in the Scriptures. Here we think, naturally, of the Ten Commandments, which are shared with Jews, Protestants, and the Orthodox. That's not terribly distinctive. Moreover, the commandments are pretty comprehensive. From them we receive moral guidance regarding the sovereignty of God and God's name; worship; honoring parents; cherishing life, our bodies, and the truth; respecting neighbors, their families, and their property. The commandments cover most moral topics.

Despite the fact that the natural law provides all human beings access to the same moral standards and that the Ten Commandments offer those of us in the Judeo-Christian tradition a fundamental morality that has affected the foundations of morality throughout the Western world, still, I say unequivocally: We Catholics have defined ourselves distinctively in our moral lives. That distinctiveness is found in the virtue of mercy.

While fellow Protestants recognize the extraordinary importance of mercy as the basic stance of our God toward us, still we Catholics have taken that insight further in terms of a long legacy of the corporal and spiritual works of mercy. Those works have distinguished us, for if there is one dimension of the Christian tradition that differentiates Protestants from Catholics, it is, precisely, "works."

I have written already on the virtues *(Virtues for Ordinary Christians)* and the Ten Commandments *(Commandments of Compassion),* two extraordinarily important influences on Catholic morality. Now I want to begin addressing the influence of the works of mercy both on our tradition and on our contemporary lives. I do this because the tradition of the works of mercy is powerfully rich, yet considerably lost to the modern mind. If we want to know more about what God asks of us today, then, assuredly it is the practice of mercy.

THE CASE FOR THE DISTINCTIVENESS OF MERCY IN THE CATHOLIC TRADITION

Mercy: The Story of Our Salvation

The Good Samaritan parable definitively defines "neighbor love" as the practice of mercy. But recall why Jesus tells this parable. He has just given the love commandment and in response, one of the scribes asks him, "Who is my neighbor?" Jesus then tells the parable. A close reading of it gives a very surprising answer to the question. Are we not thinking at the beginning of the story that the answer to the question, "Who is my neighbor?" will be *the man* lying wounded along the road. But it's not. The answer is the Samaritan. The neighbor is the one who *shows* mercy.

Like the surprising ending, many of us forget that this is not primarily a moral parable. Many great preachers and theologians see in it the first story of our redemption, told by Christ. For instance, Venerable Bede wrote that the wounded man who lies outside the gates is Adam, wounded by sin, lying outside the gates of Eden. The priest and the Levite, representing the tradition and the law, are unable to do anything for Adam. Along comes the Samaritan (Christ) who tends to Adam's wounds, takes him to the inn (the church), gives a down payment (his life) for Adam's healing (our salvation), and promises to return for him (to pay in full the cost of redemption) and take him to where he dwells (the Kingdom).

Understood in this way, the parable is less a story about how we should treat others than it is the story of what Christ has done for us. We are called to follow the actions of the Good Samaritan, not because the parable is attractive but because it is a retelling of the entire Gospel. In it, we are called to go and do likewise. The parable is not simply one among many that Jesus told. Rather, it serves as the foundational explanation of Jesus' commandment to love.

Mercy: The Condition for Salvation

My second point is that the Scriptures definitively emphasize mercy as the *condition* for salvation. This is made clear in the Last Judgment (in Matthew 25), where those saved are saved simply if they performed what we later called the corporal works of mercy—feed the hungry, give drink to the thirsty, shelter the homeless, clothe the naked, visit the sick, visit the imprisoned, and bury the dead.

The parable of Matthew 25 is striking in that everyone is surprised by the judgment. The sheep never realized that in feeding the hungry, they were feeding the king. Nor did the goats realize that by not visiting the sick, they were not visiting the Lord. But for the Gospel writers, our recognition of the importance of mercy is inconsequential. That is also the "moral" of the story of the rich man who never sees poor Lazarus at his gate. We will be judged by whether we are merciful (see Luke 6).

Mercy: The Heart of Our Theological Tradition

Our entire theological tradition is expressed in terms of mercy, which I define as the willingness to enter into the chaos of others. Indeed, like the Good Samaritan stopping for wounded Adam, attending to someone in need is no simple affair. It means entering into the entire "problem" or "chaos" of that person's particular situation.

Understood in such terms, the creation is an act of mercy that brings order into the chaos of the universe. The Incarnation is God's entry into the chaos of human existence. And the redemption is bringing us out of the chaos of our slavery to sin. Every action of God is aimed at rescuing us.

One of my favorite understandings of God's rescue of us comes from the meditation on the Trinity in the *Spiritual Exercises of Saint Ignatius.* The three persons of the blessed Trinity are considering the chaos of the world wherein most people are going to hell. They decide that we must be saved. How? One of three persons will enter into our lives to keep us all from falling into the abyss of hell, itself pure chaos.

Mercy: Christianity's Self-Definition

Early Christianity defined itself in terms of mercy. In his wonderful work *The Rise of Christianity,* Rodney Stark argues that "Christianity was an urban movement, and the New Testament was set down by urbanites." But those urban areas were dreadful. Stark describes the conditions as "social chaos and chronic urban misery," partly because of sheer population density. At the end of the first century, Antioch's population was 150,000 within the city walls—117 persons per acre. New York City today has a density of 37 persons per acre overall; Manhattan, with its high-rise apartments, registers 100 persons per acre.

Contrary to early assumptions, Greco-Roman cities were not settled places, the inhabitants descending from previous generations. Given high infant mortality and short life expectancy, these cities required "a constant and substantial stream of newcomers" simply to maintain population levels. As a result, the cities were comprised of strangers. They were well treated by Christians who, again contrary to assumptions, were anything but poor. Through a variety of ways, financially secure Christians welcomed the newly arrived immigrants.

Moreover, Christianity was new. While ethical demands were imposed by the gods of the pagan religions, these demands were substantively ritualistic, not neighbor directed. And, while pagan Romans knew generosity, it did not stem from any divine command. Thus a nurse who cared for a victim of an epidemic knew that her life might be lost. If she were a pagan, there was no expectation of divine reward for her generosity; if she were a Christian, this life was but a prelude to the next, where the generous were united with God.

Although the Romans practiced generosity, they did not promote mercy or pity. Since mercy implied "unearned help or relief," it was considered contradictory to justice. Roman philosophers opposed mercy. According to Stark, "Pity was a defect of character unworthy of the wise and excusable only in those who have not yet grown up. It was an impulsive response based on ignorance." He concludes:

> This was the moral climate in which Christianity taught that mercy is one of the primary virtues—that a merciful God requires humans to be merciful. Moreover, the corollary that *because* God loves humanity, Christians may not please God unless they *love one another* was entirely new. Perhaps even more revolutionary was the principle that Christian love and charity must extend beyond the boundaries of family and tribe, that it must extend to "all those who in every place call on the name of our Lord Jesus Christ" (1 Corinthians 1:2). This was revolutionary stuff. Indeed, it was the cultural basis for the revitalization of a Roman world groaning under a host of miseries.

In our own day, mercy makes no less a claim.

I

THE CORPORAL
WORKS OF MERCY

· 2 ·

The Corporal Works of Mercy

$\mathcal{A}$s the willingness to enter into the chaos of another, mercy best conveys the actions of God who creates by bringing order out of chaos and who redeems by lifting us out of the chaos of sin. Christ's own entrance into the chaos of death occasions our hope in the risen life. His pledge to return is a pledge to deliver us from the chaos of our own lives. Mercy is *above all* the experience we have of God.

In response to that mercy, we become imitators of the God in whose image we are made. And so, in answer to Christ's call to follow him, we practice mercy. The centrality of the practice of mercy in the life of the church cannot be overlooked. It ranks among the activities that best describe the moral life: the confessing of one's sins, obeying the Ten Commandments, developing the virtues, and practicing the corporal and spiritual works of mercy.

Much could be written about how the corporal works of mercy developed as such. We know them to be seven: feed the hungry, give drink to the thirsty, shelter the homeless, clothe the naked, visit the sick, visit the imprisoned, and bury the dead. These are later paired with the spiritual works: give good counsel, teach the ignorant, admonish sinners, console the afflicted, pardon offenses and injuries, bear offenses patiently, and pray for the living and the dead.

While the first six of the corporal works of mercy are found in the Last Judgment parable in Matthew 25:34–45, it took several centuries for the final articulation of these seven to become a cornerstone of the Christian life. Eventually they parallel other groups of seven, such as the seven sacraments, the seven deadly sins, and the virtues (four cardinal; three theological).

THE EARLY CHURCH PROMOTES THE WORKS OF MERCY

Before the set mantra of seven was firmly situated, Christians heard the divine injunction to practice mercy. John never tires of recommending it (1 John 4:20–21, for example). Luke tells us how deacons are appointed to serve the most marginalized (Acts 6:1–6). Paul writes to Timothy about the selection of widows who, like the deacons, are to serve those in need (1 Timothy 5:9–10). Collectively and institutionally the apostolic church promotes the service of mercy.

Almsgiving becomes an early expression of mercy. Clement writes, "Almsgiving is good as a penance for sin; fasting is better than prayer, but almsgiving is better than both, and charity covers a multitude of sins" (2 Clement 16). In the apostolic age, the practice of mercy is expressed in taking up a collection on the first day of every week (presumably during the Eucharist) as Paul instructs the Corinthians (1 Corinthians 16:1–2).

These many calls to mercy are heeded. For instance, Cyprian, bishop of Carthage, leads his congregation to respond to victims of the plague in 252. Bishop Dionysius provides a narrative of his community's response to the plague in Alexandria in 259. "Most of our brethren, in their surpassing charity and brotherly love did not spare themselves and clinging to one another fearlessly visited the sick and ministered to them. Many, after having nursed and consoled the sick, contracted the illness and cheerfully departed this life. The best of our brethren died in this way, some priests and deacons, and some of the laity" (Eusebius, *Hist. Eccl.* 7.22.9).

Why is the call to mercy made? Normally six motives are found in the writings of the Scriptures and among the fathers.

- First, Proverbs 15:27 encourages us to practice mercy for the remission of our sins, that is, in gratitude for God's merciful stance toward our sinfulness. John Chrysostom sees mercy, in this passage, as the queen of the virtues, outweighing all our burdensome sins.
- Second, Tobit 12:8–9 tells us that for our prayers to be heard by God, works of mercy should accompany them. Several of the fathers, Augustine, Cyprian, Leo the Great, and John Chrysostom, preach on this theme.
- Third, Matthew 6:20 suggests that works of mercy will lead to eternal reward, a motivation that Augustine often uses.

- Fourth, no less than Matthew 25:40 reveals to us that any merciful action is for the sake of the Lord. Cyprian calls this the most powerful of all motives. Here, many of the fathers promote the figures of Mary of Bethany and Zacchaeus as models of mercy. Similarly, the celebrated episode of Martin of Tours giving his cloak to the beggar becomes a motif throughout the church.
- Fifth, Lactantius and Ambrose urge mercy to fortify human solidarity and to extend the circle of fellowship in the Lord.
- Finally, Clement of Alexandria, John Chrysostom, and Leo the Great remind us that works of mercy bring us into the life of perfection. By practicing mercy we become more like the God who entered into our own chaos.

THE MIDDLE AGES AND THE RENAISSANCE

In the Middle Ages, the monasteries become centers for extraordinary mercy. One account from the famed monastery at Cluny, for instance, informs us that seventeen thousand persons are cared for in one year. Among the Cistercians, every abbey has a guest house for pilgrims, travelers, and the poor where the abbot waits on them, after first welcoming them by prostrating himself at their feet.

Besides the monks, pious laypersons participate in the works of mercy by forming "lay associations." These begin in Naples in the tenth century and later appear in Tuscany. By the twelfth century they are throughout France, Spain, and Italy, assisting members of religious orders in their apostolates mostly by establishing and maintaining hospitals. For instance, in 1217, a hospital that once belonged to a religious community is handed over to a corporation of four priests, thirty laymen, and twenty-five laywomen. By the thirteenth and fourteenth century these activities are flourishing throughout Europe.

With the spirit of Francis and Dominic in the thirteenth century, many professional laypersons become inspired and answer the call to mercy with great imagination. For instance, in 1244, the head porter of a wool guild in Florence (Pier Luca Borsi) forms the Company of Mercy with money collected by taxing colleagues for swearing. Others reach out to those suffering from leprosy. The Knights of St. Lazarus alone established three thousand hospitals for those suffering from the dreaded disease. Later hospitals for the blind and foundlings for orphans are also founded.

One effect of the Crusades is the widespread practice of prostitution. In its aftermath, foundations are established to provide sanctuaries to the women; in turn, the women form religious congregations. In the thirteenth century, for instance, the Congregation of the Penitents of St. Mary Magdalen has thirty communities throughout Europe.

By the sixteenth century, the establishment of guilds along with the innovations of new religious orders like the Jesuits, as well as the important reforms of the Council of Trent, provide new impetus for laypersons to belong to confraternities, the successor of "lay associations." In the next seven chapters I shall examine these confraternities, which wedded spiritual growth and devotion with the practice of mercy. Here I mention only two. The Company of Divine Love is established to respond to those with syphilis, which breaks out throughout Europe in the mid-1490s. Sufferers from this incurable disease are abandoned both by families because of shame and by hospitals because of fear of contagion. In 1499 the first hospital for the incurables is built in Genoa, then another in Rome, and others in Naples, Venice, and finally throughout Europe. The company heralded the continent's response of compassion to those afflicted by the awful disease.

In 1498 Queen Eleanor of Portugal establishes the Confraternity of Misericordia. In 1516 it has one hundred members: fifty from the nobility, fifty from the working class, all dedicated to the fourteen works of mercy. By the queen's death in 1525 there are sixty-one branches of the confraternity. From the seventeenth to the nineteenth century, twenty-five confraternities are established in Portuguese colonies. Many still stand today.

We cannot underestimate the relevance of these confraternities: Hundreds of them take care of prisoners and captives; others are established for the care of the mentally ill as well as those who are unable to hear and/or speak. These confraternities are only paralleled by the extraordinary number of religious orders which themselves adopt a work of mercy to identify with their own charism.

CONCLUSION

Today many persons speak of the emerging lay ministry. But during a variety of periods in the church's life, laypersons—animated both by their own God-given talents and by the fundamental experience of God's mercy—were ministers. Their legacy of leadership and service needs to be studied, for it was phenomenal. A proper place to find it is in the variety of lay associations and confraternities in both the medieval and Renaissance periods. In those times of spiritual richness and economic prosperity, times like our own, the laity, alongside clergy and religious, imitated the merciful ways of the Good Samaritan.

• 3 •

Visit the Prisoner

$\mathcal{S}$r. Maureen Clark, C.S.J., has been working in prison ministry for many years and currently visits, supports, listens to, and works with the women at the women's correctional facility in Framingham, Massachusetts. Recently, she was looking for new clergy to preside at Sunday Mass and one of her volunteer musicians, a doctoral student of mine, promptly volunteered me. My schedule is busy. But I decided that I wanted to go.

Having grown up as the son of a New York City police detective, prisons have always been frightening places for me. They became more terrifying when my dad, who later became involved in the investigation of the Attica uprising, took me through Attica. As I walked through the cavernous, gray hallways, I became afraid that by some accident I would be left inside.

Years later, while visiting a Jesuit friend in southern California, he informed me that we were going to Tijuana to say Mass in the city jail. He told me that this was the happiest task of his priestly ministry, even though he described the place as very confining and very chaotic and didn't hesitate to let me know the broad diversity of crimes—from petty debts to kidnapping and murder—for which these men had been detained. I remember entering the cell with all the fear of a young child, watching my friend greet, embrace, and chat with the prisoners, mingling while I rigidly stood by the makeshift altar, occasionally glancing (almost frantically) at the guards on the other side of the cage. The strongest memory I have of that place is that when the liturgy was over, the guards announced that they could not open the gates to let us out for another twenty to thirty minutes. My friend smiled, shrugged his shoulders, and went back to the prisoners. I stayed by the doors and waited.

The invitation to Framingham was not, then, what I would have put on my annual wish list. Yet, in light of the many fears that I have had to face, I thought, why not this one, too. The situation would be different, after all. I would be in Framingham, not Tijuana nor Attica.

I met Sr. Maureen and about twenty volunteers (who were among a group of about a hundred) who take turns coming to the Sunday evening Mass. They led me through the procedures. I had to leave my wallet, wristwatch, car keys, and cash in the lockers. I had to sign in. Then I had to wait nearly an hour. I was searched and eventually allowed to pass through innumerable gates and doors to go to the room where the Mass would be held.

The Mass itself was extraordinarily consoling. The women were welcoming. Several hundred showed up. They set up the altar, checked the readings, joined the choir, or just sat and prayed. They wanted to pray, especially for their children and, yes, grandchildren, as well as for their sister inmates. Their prayers were many and they enjoyed the liturgy.

But they were in prison.

Whatever personal freedom I had gained by facing my fear, I realized that their freedom was incredibly restricted. I especially understood this when one woman prayed for another younger woman who was to go to a hearing the next day. The hearing was to determine whether she could be released early. There was an evident, but quiet desperation on the faces of many as this prayer was uttered.

"Do you like this work?" I later asked Maureen. "I love these women," she answered.

PRISON MINISTRY: A HISTORICAL SKETCH

After celebrating his first papal Christmas Mass at St. Peter's, John XXIII went, without any prior notification, to Rome's children's hospital, Gésu Bambino, to visit the children there. The next day, December 26, John XXIII again left Vatican City to visit the prisoners of Regina Coeli. He arrived, explaining, "You could not come to see me so I have come to see you."

This remarkable event is today recorded in bronze on the central doors of St. Peter's Basilica in the extraordinary work of Giacomo

Manzú. There in the middle of the left panel is Pope John XXIII, stretching his hands through prison bars, grasping the prisoners' hands while calling them his brothers.

Visiting prisoners has always been a corporal work of mercy practiced by Christians throughout the life of the church. Inasmuch as they were persecuted, church members visited their imprisoned brothers and sisters and worked to liberate them. Like Tertullian, Cyprian, and others, St. Ignatius of Antioch writes about such visits. In his Letter to the Christians of Smyrna, Ignatius writes, "When the Christians become aware that one of their number is a prisoner and suffering for the name of Christ, they take upon themselves all his needs and, if possible, they free him."

Early Christians routinely sought to comfort their fellow Christians who were imprisoned; they sought their blessing as well. Christ himself had been a prisoner. Thus, like Peter, Paul, and many of the apostles, imprisoned Christians were perceived as not only people in need but also people of courage and holiness. Working to visit, console, and liberate them was in itself its own reward.

Clement of Rome tells us in his first chapter to the Corinthians that many Christians ransomed others by offering themselves in exchange for the one held hostage. No less than Pope Paul VI followed this example when he offered himself to Italy's Red Brigade in exchange for the Roman mayor, Aldo Moro. (The pope's offer was quickly rejected and the beloved Moro was found murdered in the trunk of a car.)

During the twelfth century, a time of enormous spiritual and ecclesial development, charitable institutions were established for the release of prisoners. The Trinitarians, founded by St. John of Matha, were singularly dedicated to ransoming prisoners and laboring to alleviate the conditions of those who remained in slavery. Similarly, the Order of Mercy was founded by St. Peter Nolasco for the same task.

In another period of spiritual renewal, the sixteenth century, religious orders were founded whose members worked, among other ministries, for the care and release of prisoners. The Jesuits, for instance, provided a variety of such services. In *The First Jesuits,* historian John O'Malley reminds us first who these prisoners were: either debtors or those awaiting trial, sentencing, or execution. In Rome, over half the imprisoned were debtors from the poorer classes; the others, awaiting trial, had not yet had their guilt established. Jesuits took care of the imprisoned by preaching, catechizing, and confessing the imprisoned and by bring-ing them food and alms. In Italy and Spain, Jesuits spent a great deal of time raising funds through begging so as to pay off the prisoners' credi-tors. Elsewhere they begged for money to ransom back prisoners taken by the Turks. They also preached against slave-taking raids.

Sometimes the Jesuits worked to improve the plight of prisons. In Palermo, for instance, a confraternity was founded, based on one Jesuit's work to improve the sanitary conditions of prisoners. Another confrater-nity organized by the Jesuits, the Confraternity of the Imprisoned, was founded for laypersons in Rome. It generated other confraternities in six more cities throughout Italy.

Other confraternities of the laity dedicated themselves to those in prison. In Rome, the Archconfraternity of Charity was specifically for those in captivity, as was the Confraternity of the Pietà and Our Lady of Loreto in Milan. In France, confraternities such as the Work of Prisons in Marseilles and the Confraternity of Mercy in Lyons were dedicated solely to prisoners' needs, while the White Penitents and the Sisters of the Dominican Third Order were dedicated singularly to the needs of women prisoners.

From such experiences of the prisons, a number of critical voices rose, protesting conditions and starting reform movements to correct conditions among prisoners in Spain, Italy, France, and England.

REFORM MOVEMENTS

The need to reform or abolish prisons is perennial and universal. The specific need to look at prison life in the United States was brought to light recently in an extraordinary article in *Theological Studies* by Patrick McCormick. McCormick, analyzing the "justice" of the U.S. criminal justice system, begins with several noteworthy statistics. Here are a few:

- Between 1972 and 1998 the population of our state and federal prisons more than sextupled, growing from less than 200,000 to over 1.2 million.
- By mid-1999, the total U.S. prison and jail population totaled 1,860,520 and is expected to pass 2,000,000 by the end of 2001.

- Our national incarceration rate (682 per 100,000) is only slightly behind the world's leading jailer, Russia (685 per 100,000).
- The United States has 500,000 more prisoners than China does.
- About a quarter of all the world's prisoners are in the United States.
- Half of all inmates are African American.
- Nationwide, one out of every three young African American males are in the criminal justice system.
- In 1970 there were slightly more than 5,600 women in prisons across the United States. By 1996 there were nearly 75,000, a thirteen-fold increase.
- The majority of this increase consisted of women arrested for nonviolent crimes.
- African American women are the fastest growing demographic group among the newly incarcerated.

Visiting prisoners inevitably leads to a recognition of the need for prison reform. The call for prison reform has been made from a variety of sectors, but two recent ones are particularly noteworthy. The New York State Catholic Conference's "Statement on Drug Sentencing Reform" (June 14, 1999) calls upon the New York State Legislature to repeal the Rockefeller drug laws, which many recognize as inaugurating automatic sentencing. Likewise, in November the U.S. bishops voted unanimously in favor of the document from Archbishop Roger Mahony's Committee on Domestic Policy, "Responsibility, Rehabilitation, and Restoration: A Catholic Perspective on Crime and Criminal Justice." Reading that comprehensive statement, any contemporary Catholic could grasp the urgent call for reform in the criminal justice system.

Visiting prisoners has always been a corporal work of mercy. Prisons have always existed, isolating those often most in need. Today's statistics suggest that more and more of those in need are being held captive. John XXIII understood as much when he hastened to the prisoners, saying, "You could not come to see me so I have come to see you." In light of the dreadful situation in the United States (and elsewhere), this corporal work of mercy is no quaint practice, but rather a necessary, even urgent one. It prompts us to look for the persons most isolated and to build bridges to them. It invites us to receive their blessings. And it awakens us, as such visits have always done, to find ways of liberating the captive, a biblical command.

• 4 •

Shelter the Homeless

$\mathcal{I}$s it not striking that the two infancy narratives of the Gospels concern the need to shelter the Christ child?

The Old Testament begins with the creation of the heavens and their many stars, and the earth and its lands and seas with their multitudinous varieties of species of life. The creation culminates with man and woman, who are given care of the entire world. The Creator is bountiful; the Creator's world becomes our world; the Creator's home, our home. We the newly arrived become the caretaker's host of the new world. We lack nothing. Everything is abundant in Genesis.

Yet while the Old Testament begins with the display of God's hospitality, the New Testament begins with the jarring depictions of the profoundly inhospitable environments in which the Christ child finds himself. Luke's Gospel describes Mary and Joseph unable to find even an inn in which the child could be born. As opposed to the beauty in which Adam and Eve find themselves at the beginning of their lives, the squalor of the setting of Jesus' birth is not incidental. The stable in Bethlehem is a long way from the Garden of Eden. Matthew's Gospel is even less forgiving. The infant's parents have to flee their homeland to save the child's life. Their own land is so profoundly inhospitable that they become refugees in the land of those who once oppressed their people.

Throughout the Gospels, however, the adult Jesus unfailingly preaches hospitality, admonishing the disciples to tend to the needs of others, whether they be children or hungry listeners. Fittingly, the most poignant hospitable action of Jesus takes place as he hangs on the cross, promising "the good thief" that he will be with him in his Father's kingdom (Luke 23:42–43).

21

A LONG TRADITION OF WELCOMING THE STRANGER

Emulating Jesus' example and teaching, the early church urged the practice of hospitality. Paul writes to the Romans, "Share the needs of the saints, practicing hospitality" (Romans 12:13). Peter urges, "Be hospitable to one another without murmuring" (1 Peter 4:9). The writer of the Letter to the Hebrews reminds us of the stories of Lot and Sodom and warns us "to not forget to entertain strangers; for thereby some have entertained angels unawares" (Hebrews 13:2). Likewise, Cyprian (*Letter* 7) and Tertullian (*To Wives* 2:4), as well as the writers of the Didache (12) and the *Shepherd of Hermas* (8:10), all urge Christians to practice the hospitality of sheltering the stranger. Clement often recommends it (1 Corinthians 1:2, 10:7, 11:1, 12:1) and Melito, bishop of Sardis, writes a treatise on it, *Peri filoxenias.* In fact, Rome's fame in Christendom was not primarily based on its being the center of apostolic activity; rather, it was the source of such generous benefaction.

After the edict of Constantine, the church's bishops began institutional practices of hospitality. For instance, after a famine struck Cesarea of Cappadocia (in 378), Basil constructed on the boundaries of the city a set of buildings to receive travelers and the sick, especially lepers.

Later, the Rule of Benedict provided a great impetus for the development of other institutional responses to shelter the stranger. Benedict dedicated chapter 53 of his Rule to hospitality and provided two different structures to respond to those in need. The guest house was designed for persons of means; it provided welcome, stability, and shelter for pilgrims, monks, nobles, and clergy. By contrast, the hospice received persons in dire need—beggars, invalids, the aged, and infirm.

These distinctions later evolved into other expressions, but providing shelter to the homeless continued to be identified with Benedictine charism. The monastery of Cluny became a model of reform and of hospitality. The Cistercians, likewise, followed suit; every Cistercian abbey had its guest house. In a Cistercian guest house in Fossanova, the exhausted Thomas Aquinas collapsed and died.

While the Benedictines practiced hospitality outside the medieval town walls, by the twelfth and thirteenth centuries the Canon Regulars practiced it within the center of civic life, providing structures to care for pilgrims, the sick, pregnant women, widows, and orphans. As we can see, the needs of women, especially widows, occasioned these responses. The feminization of poverty is not a new phenomenon.

These institutions were raised to respond to specific persons in need. Earlier, I mentioned that one of the results of the extraordinary upheaval created by the Crusades was the rapid spread of prostitution. After the Crusades, prostitutes were without funds and shelter. By the end of the twelfth century, houses of refuge were established in Bologna, Paris, Marseilles, Messina, and Rome. In turn, some of these prostitutes themselves became sponsors of hospitality. Founding the Congregation of the Penitents of St. Mary Magdalen (1225), these women established fifty houses throughout Europe, providing community life for their members and shelter for prostitutes in need.

Similarly, in the twelfth century people living near mountains, forests, and rivers became aware of travelers and pilgrims passing their way. Not only did these residents offer shelter for the wayfarers, but they became alert to their specific problems. Some residents became regional guides for the travelers, while others became bridge builders. By the thirteenth century, associations for the maintenance of roads and bridges were established in a variety of locations throughout western and central Europe.

In the fifteenth century, Christians established the first of many orphanages; the Hospital of the Innocents became a refuge center for foundlings.

This appreciation of shelters for different populations prompted Anthony of Florence, who authored the first treatise on the corporal works of mercy, to distinguish four different shelters: for the poor and pilgrims, for the elderly, for orphans, and for nourishing infants.

CONTEMPORARY PEOPLES IN NEED

As we have seen, entering into the chaos of those who need shelter usually requires recognition of a particular population. Otherwise, we cannot develop the necessary services to attend to their needs. Today three particular populations capture our attention.

1. Refugees

Currently there are forty-five million refugees and displaced persons around the world. Within that enormous population, 80 percent are women and children. Catholic Relief Services and Caritas Internationalis dedicate themselves to the diverse needs of this group. Similarly, the Jesuits follow the practice of their Benedictine forerunners by administering the Jesuit Refugee Service worldwide.

2. *Adolescent Runaways*

Throughout the world there is an enormous population of adolescent runaways. Covenant House, the largest privately funded child-care agency in the United States, provides shelter and service to homeless and runaway youth. Incorporated in New York City in 1972, it has since expanded within the United States (to Anchorage, Atlantic City, Detroit, Fort Lauderdale, Houston, Los Angeles, Newark, New Orleans, Oakland, Orlando, Philadelphia, St. Louis, and Washington, D.C.) and outside it (to Toronto, Vancouver, Guatemala, Honduras, Mexico, and Nicaragua).

Covenant House provided residential and nonresidential services to over fifty thousand youth in 2000. More than thirteen thousand young people came to Covenant House Crisis Shelters and Rights of Passage Programs. Another sixteen thousand received help in Community Service centers or in aftercare and prevention services. And their outreach workers served nearly twenty-one thousand youth on the street.

3. *Women*

Although our awareness of the needs of this population is only emerging, many, many poor women are in need of shelter. The first emergency shelter for poor women in the United States was Rosie's Place, founded in 1974, when Kip Tiernan, a Boston activist, noticed that women were disguising themselves as men in order to obtain shelter. Today, Rosie's Place has evolved from simply providing shelter to offering relief, from the immediate to the long term. Their programs include serving lunch and dinner every day; offering emergency shelter and permanent housing; engaging in advocacy; providing a clothing center and food pantry; developing a food cooperative; supplying job training ("Women's Craft Cooperative"); and more. Rosie's Place strives to provide a safe and nurturing environment to help poor and homeless women maintain their dignity, seek opportunity, and find security in their lives. The Catholic Worker houses, started by Dorothy Day and Peter Maurin, also take in women as well as men. New York's Mary House is a residence for women, while Joseph House shelters men.

Some of the women and children seeking shelter are victims of domestic violence. Poor women who receive welfare benefits may be abused by their male partners. Recent studies show that an astonishing 60 percent of these women have been physically abused (one definition of "abused" is "slapped at least six times, kicked, bit, hit with a fist, hit with an object, beaten up, or more injurious acts") during their adult lives, and 20 percent are currently in abusive situations.

Victims of domestic violence are sheltered across the nation, from Las Casas de las Madres in San Francisco and the Women's Transition House in Victoria to Safe Haven Ministries in Michigan and St. Martha's Hall in St. Louis to Florida's Clay County Quigley House and the House of Ruth in Washington, D.C. As society continues to combat with powerful messages the profound wrongness of domestic violence, these interim shelters witness to the urgent need to combat it.

People of diverse religious backgrounds often work together to shelter diverse populations in need. Trying to find out where we can assist in this corporal work of mercy, we need only turn to any diocesan Catholic Charities. In the Archdiocese of New York, for example, Catholic Charities continues the long tradition of caring for orphans by administering the 131-year-old Foundling Hospital. Boys Hope, Good Shepherd Services, Mission of the Immaculate Virgin, and St. Cabrini homes are but a few of the residential services for adolescents in need of support and shelter. Catholic Home, Mitty, and Seton Residences are a few of the facilities that shelter women with children, specifically.

In sheltering the homeless, we participate in a long tradition of mercy. We meet those most in need of being incorporated into a world that, since the days of Eden, has had to work to provide hospitality and a safe haven.

Feed the Hungry

$\mathscr{F}$eeding the hungry is almost always associated with entering into fellowship with another. This is not surprising since eating itself is the most ordinary and fundamental way that Jesus celebrates his fellowship with us. The Last Supper is the lasting testimony of Jesus' promise to eat one day with us all. And the significance of that testimony is what we celebrate in the Eucharist.

THE SCRIPTURES

Not surprisingly, Jesus preaches that the kingdom of heaven is a great banquet. In fact, Jesus often plays with us about our tendency not to recognize who will be included in that messianic banquet. In Luke's Gospel he preaches that the unexpected people from the byways will be brought into the feast (Luke 5:34). Likewise, when he preaches to the masses, Jesus expects to conclude his meeting with them in a meal. The disciples never grasp this, wishing instead to send the listeners away hungry. But Jesus brings them into his table fellowship by his magnificent multiplication of loaves feeding the five thousand (the only miracle to appear in all four Gospels: John 6:1–15; Matthew 14:13–21; Mark 6:32–44; and Luke 9:10–17). In addition to the feeding, the miracle yields an extra twelve baskets as a simple reminder of the banquet to be celebrated again at the end of time when he will gather us into the twelve tribes of Israel. John's Gospel takes the miracle's significance even further by following it with his own discourse on the identity between Jesus and the bread that will sustain us for all time: "I am the bread who has come down from heaven" (John 6:41).

The great scandal for Christians, then, is to ignore the needs of the hungry. For just as Jesus trains his disciples to feed the hungry—see the feeding of the four thousand (Matthew 15:32–39; Mark 8:1–10)—so he warns us all against ignoring the needs of the hungry.

No story hits us harder than the one of the rich man who wants only to be relieved of his eternal suffering (Luke 16:19–31). While we may think that his was a just sentence since he ignored the plight of Lazarus who lay at his gate and "who desired to be fed with what fell from the rich man's table," still we must recognize that the rich man did not maliciously withhold his "crumbs" from Lazarus. He simply did not recognize Lazarus and his needs. Lazarus is not a part of the rich man's fellowship; a gulf exists between them that Lazarus was not welcome to traverse. Unfortunately, in the next life, the rich man will not be able to traverse the gulf either.

Later, the first great dissension for the early church concerns eating and inclusion. The Greek-speakers claimed that their widows were being neglected, a charge that led to the appointment of "the seven" (Acts 6:1–6). Likewise, disorder at table fellowship and the failure to leave enough food for latecomers became an issue for Paul in his letter to the Corinthians (1 Corinthians 11:33–34). The widows, like the latecomers, could have become another Lazarus had the communities been unaware of their needs. In recognizing their needs, however, they recognized that eating and inclusion are mutually defining matters in the life of the church.

THE TRADITION

The intimate relationship between food and inclusion is seen in the life of the church as we celebrate Advent and Lent, when in recognition of the gift of our redemption, we engage in the two practices of fasting (in order to acknowledge our unworthiness) and almsgiving (so as to incorporate better those from the margins of our society). The two practices are as intimately related to each another as are food and inclusion.

One of the more interesting accounts of the relationship between food and inclusion is told by Caroline Walker Bynum in her landmark study *Holy Feast and Holy Fast: The Religious Significance of Food to Medieval Women*. Bynum recounts how women of deep faith understood themselves as embodied just as Christ was. Separated from the access to communion that priests had, women encountered in their own flesh the body of Christ that was so hard to receive from their male counterparts. In their bodies through fasting, ascetical practices, stigmata, mystical visions, and even mystical unions, women experienced the suffering and redeeming body of Christ. Full incorporation was found precisely in and through the body in its feasting and fasting.

Similarly in later centuries, church organizations made the connection between eating and inclusion. It was a common event, for instance, for the confraternities of the Renaissance to celebrate feasts by extending their table fellowship to those among the poorest. Likewise, confraternities, such as Genoa's Confraternity of the Most Holy Sacrament, specifically concerned themselves with bringing Communion to those who were sick so as to incorporate them through the Eucharist. The church has always recognized the need to remember Lazarus at the gates.

In a much more contemporary way we see the relationship between eating and inclusion in the annual celebration of Thanksgiving. On that day churches around the nation celebrate meals where parishioners sit down together with Lazarus. Like the original day itself, on which the Puritans and the Native Americans shared table fellowship, the feast is not only a day of eating, it is a day of being included at the one table of thanksgiving.

Similarly, soup kitchens today often insist that volunteers not only prepare and serve a meal, but also that they eat it, breaking bread with those whom they serve. In Unity Kitchen of Syracuse, for instance, no one could offer any assistance, even the donation of food, unless he or she did so when the kitchen was serving Lazarus in need.

TODAY

Almost all charitable organizations that address the needs of Lazarus recognize the importance of inclusivity. Oxfam America (http://www.oxfamamerica.org) mentions it in the organization's simple mission statement:

> Oxfam America is dedicated to creating lasting solutions to hunger, poverty, and social injustice through long-term partnerships with poor communities around the world. As a privately funded organization, we can speak with conviction and integrity as we challenge the structural barriers that foster conflict and human suffering and limit people from gaining the skills, resources, and power to become self-sufficient.

Oxfam claims that "the distinctiveness of our partnerships is defined by mutual respect and a willingness to be innovative, share risks, and assume long-term relationships."

But why, if food is the answer to people's hunger, do relief workers still insist on inclusivity? Shouldn't we be concerned with whether Lazarus is eating rather than with whether he is eating with us? Is the concern of relief workers simply an attempt to imitate a pious insight from the Bible? Or is there some effective political relevance to this bond between inclusivity and food? The answers can be easily found in two wonderful booklets (*Food* by Josanthony Joseph and *Famine* by Michael Drumm) published through Ireland's Veritas House by the United Kingdom's Catholic Fund for Overseas Development (CAFOD: http://www.cafod.org.uk) and Ireland's Catholic Agency for World Development (Trocaire: http://www.trocaire.org).

Here we find extraordinary data: some 824 million people are underfed, of whom 790 million are in the developing world; 40 percent of all children in South Asia and 33 percent in sub-Saharan Africa still go hungry. Are these people hungry because of food shortages?

In 1997, an American Association for the Advancement of Science study revealed that 78 percent of all malnourished children in the developing world live in countries with food surpluses. In fact, as Josanthony Joseph points out, "the world's food production has outstripped population growth by about 16 percent over the last 35 years." Joseph adds that during the Ethiopian famine of 1984, that country used some of its best farmland to grow animal feed for export to Europe. Similarly, in 1995, India exported five million tons of rice and hundreds of millions of dollars worth of wheat and flour when more than one in five Indians went hungry.

Joseph concludes, "What is clear is that food insecurity can never be explained by population density and a resultant inadequacy of food stocks. Instead people are hungry because they lack resources to access food through the cash economy." The answer to hunger is found in access.

Like Oxfam, CAFOD, and Trocaire, Catholic Relief Services (CRS) is an organization dedicated to answering the needs of the hungry by bringing them into physical and economic access to sufficient food. According to its website (http://www.catholicrelief.org), CRS works in nearly eighty countries worldwide. To illustrate the type of work it promotes, CRS lists nearly twenty regional projects designed to bridge the gap between the rest of society and those marginalized by economic barriers, social class structures, or other obstacles that leave them outside the circle of the human community:

> We understand ourselves to be part of a wider global family and believe that our responsibilities to one another cross national, cultural and religious boundaries. Our work worldwide is a concrete expression of the interdependence of all people in community with each other as we seek to fulfill our responsibilities to our brothers and sisters worldwide.

When we bring people into fellowship, we bring them into a sharing of the fruits of the harvest.

Every Sunday we gather at the table of the Lord to celebrate our redemption through the body and blood of Christ. As we partake in that feast we need to ask ourselves where Lazarus is as we gather. For Lazarus is at the gates. Somehow we need to bring him closer to the table, for his own good and for ours.

· 6 ·

Give Drink to the Thirsty

$\mathcal{L}$ast summer I returned from ten weeks of teaching in the Loyola School of Theology at the Ateneo de Manila in the Philippines. I had a wonderful time teaching two courses to the many divinity students there. They, like the rest of the people I met around Manila, were warm, hospitable, and terribly interested in moving their great nation forward.

Living there for ten weeks during monsoon season, I became accustomed to water! My first week preceded the rains. For several mornings I had great runs on a track at the highest point of the beautiful campus. But by the third week, after several monsoons and one typhoon, the track, like the entire country, became, well, soggy. Fortunately, I found an indoor track at the university gym.

Every night, almost like clockwork, heavy rains fell. The density of the rainfall was as impressive as the sound of the water beating against thick palm branches. After the nightly rains, the campus became luscious with new vegetation and flowers.

I often wondered how the poorer people, who lived in shanties nearby, fared. Their homes were not completely insulated from the rains. And with the rainfall so constant, few periods lasted long enough even for clothing to dry. If I couldn't get my pants and shoes to dry, how could they dry out their homes?

Despite all this rain, people still lacked water. I often saw poorer people take advantage of the rainfall by showering along the roadside, soaping themselves down. Not only did they lack indoor plumbing, but they had no way of retaining enough rainfall to wash themselves or their clothing with any predictable regularity.

33

Inadequate drinking water posed a bigger problem for some. The Jesuits, for instance, who lived in the valley adjoining the campus, routinely arrived at school with water jugs to take back potable water. They faced the possibility of either dangerous amoebas or toxins being in their drinking water.

THE NEED FOR AVAILABLE CLEAN WATER

These stories from the Philippines may help us to appreciate the fact that the presence of water (as in rainfall) does not guarantee the presence of suitable water. Finding adequate water for washing, cooking, and drinking is much more complicated than drawing a bucket of water from a well.

I know this firsthand from another summer, when I studied Spanish in the Dominican Republic. In the tropics, there is plenty of water, but little of it can be used as drinking water. During a weekend traveling around the countryside, we repeatedly asked wherever we stopped whether the water was "purified." At the very last place we visited, someone in our group insisted that we not ask because, as he said, "Obviously in a place like this, they purify the water." He was wrong. And several days later I was a patient at the major hospital in Santiago.

Campaigns for accessible clean water are perennial. One need only consult websites of the World Health Organization or the Pan American Health Organization to appreciate the needs throughout the world for clean water. Unfortunately, when those needs are not met, cholera and dysentery break out. Then we see even more clearly how precious clean water really is.

In the United States and Canada, too, concerns about clean water arise. Sixteen years ago, for example, *Church* magazine published a report of the presentation by Bishop Raymond Peña of El Paso, Texas, to the House Committee on Public Works (Summer 1988). The bishop said, "Few expect anything other than pure, clean water to be available to them in their homes: for drinking, for cooking, for bathing, for washing their clothes. Yet there are many for whom clean water in their homes is only a dream." Peña added, "I assure you that the problem you address here today is not a rare one. It is found in Laredo in the Diocese of Corpus Christi, throughout the valley in the Diocese of Brownsville, and in El Paso."

In that same issue, Pat Coyle wrote about Southern Maryland Area Self-Help (SMASH), an organization that worked to bring running water into the homes of over a thousand families in Charles County and another seven hundred families in Prince George's County. As Coyle noted, these homes were a mere thirty miles from the White House.

THE WORK OF THE NATIONAL
CATHOLIC RURAL LIFE CONFERENCE

The problems of sixteen years ago are, unfortunately, not unlike the problems we face today. We need only turn to the National Catholic Rural Life Conference website (http://www.ncrlc.com) to find its ingenious educational campaign, "Eating is a moral act." In a series of six lessons, the conference makes clear that "our water is at risk." Water, it insists, is "integral to a healthy web of life."

The conference helps us to see that the call to give drink to the thirsty is itself the call to develop an attitude that respects the needs of those who are poor and that appreciates the gifts of the earth. We need to realize that the way we treat our land, whether in urban or rural areas, eventually redounds to all of us. The web of life requires a harmonious estimation of both ourselves and our planet: Where we harm our planet, we eventually harm ourselves. Inevitably, justice affects us all.

In a talk entitled "Water and Wisdom in the Web of Life," Brother David Andrews, C.S.C., executive director of the conference, helps us appreciate just how dependent we are on water. We already know that water is all around us, that our planet and our atmosphere are literally filled with water. But Andrews helps us to see that water is not simply around us, it constitutes us! "Modern science tells us that water is the stuff of life; 75 percent of each of us and most living things is water. It is said that at birth we are 90 percent water. We dry as we age until, by maturity, our bodies are about 70 percent water and our blood 83 percent. When we eat, our food must be dissolved in liquid in our digestive systems before it can be absorbed into our bodies. Much of our food is high in water content: a potato contains 80 percent, an apple 85 percent, tomatoes and lettuce 95 percent, a watermelon 97 percent."

Andrews doubts, however, our willingness to appreciate this fact. Rather, he insists that the earth today is among "the oppressed." He calls, for instance, for an immediate halt on the construction of factory farms, which he labels "the contemporary equivalent of Chernobyl and Three Mile Island," because they are destroying communities, livelihoods, a way of life, and the environment. Instead, Andrews suggests alternatives that are sustainable, effective, and compatible with the land, water, air, and human communities.

This corporal work of mercy, in a manner of speaking, is the one that calls us to attend to developing a more environmentally sensitive form of spirituality. Inevitably such an asceticism is, as we have seen, in our own interest. Thus, Andrews offers us a way of developing an appreciation for the world's gifts, especially water. He tells two stories that capture in their simplicity the type of dispositions that we need to develop today.

In New Mexico, Jim Chee, a Navaho police officer, is having a cup of coffee in his trailer. Unlike the homes of his ancestors, Chee's trailer has running water. When he finishes his coffee and rinses out his cup, he drinks the rinse water. A people who have lived for centuries in a dry and arid land know how precious water is.

In Korea, Zen Buddhist monks gather for a meal of water, rice, and soup. Each monk has four bowls in front of him. He receives water into the largest bowl; divides that water between the next two bowls, and stores the residue in the smallest bowl. When the meal is over, rice water is served, and with it the monk rinses out the rice bowl, and then the soup bowl and side-dish bowl. After these three bowls are rinsed, the monk drinks the rinse water. He then puts the clean water he had stored in the small water bowl into his rice bowl and cleans it by hand. He follows by cleaning his other two bowls. The wastewater is poured into a bucket. It must be perfectly clear; otherwise the monk will have to drink it too. The wastewater is offered to ghosts whose mouths are so tiny they are hurt by even small particles of food.

Like these religious people, we too must develop internal and external practices that help us to respect our environment, particularly water and our universal dependence on it. Perhaps, a start is to consider prayerfully the meaning of the biblical call to give drink to the thirsty.

· 7 ·

Bury the Dead

EARLY CHRISTIAN PRACTICES

Since the days of the early church, Christians have buried the dead. Following the Jewish customs, Christians interred their dead and rejected any attempts to cremate. As Christianity grew, it developed burial rituals that reflected a theology emphasizing the goodness of creation, the redemption of embodied lives, and the resurrection of the human body.

While pagans acknowledged the moment of the death of the loved one with *conclamatio,* or violent outcry of grief, Christians quietly recited prayers and psalms to accompany the deceased into their period of transition. Shortly afterward they washed the newly dead body (see the death of Dorcas, Acts 9:37). Then, after an anointing of the body to preserve it for burial, they wrapped it in linen. This wrapping repeats the practice of wrapping the newly baptized, an action that in both cases symbolizes a body wrapped for glory. Then the body was dressed in clothes to identify the deceased person's state of life. Here the church emphasized the sense of continuity between earthly and heavenly life; belief in the resurrection of the body means that we expect to be in heaven who we have been on earth.

During the wake, the body was surrounded by candles to symbolize the perpetual light to which the deceased was called. After the wake came an emphatically triumphant funeral procession, which stood in marked contrast to the rituals of pagans wherein groups of mourners, including those hired, expressed deep sighs of grief. Alfred Rush, the author of *Death and Burial in Christian Antiquity,* notes that the early Christian participants in burial processions joyfully sang psalms. Writes St. John Chrysostom in the fourth century: "Is it not that we praise God and

37

thank Him that he has crowned the departed and freed him from suffering, and that God has the deceased, now free from fear, with Himself?"

A Eucharistic celebration, either at the church or the grave, followed the procession. Someone delivered a eulogy, emphasizing both the life of the loved one and the consolation of the Christian faith. The liturgy concluded with relatives giving a final kiss to the body of the deceased. It expressed the affection of the mourners and their belief in the sacredness of the body. Rush notes that this kiss appalled believers from other contemporary religions, who thought that any contact with the corpse was an act of defilement.

For the interment, the body was buried facing the east, expressing the expectation of the second coming of Christ in glory. Rush notes that while originally there was no direct link between burial in the ground and resurrection, the practice came to be seen as a natural corollary to the image of a seed being planted.

Commemoration of loved ones was celebrated not on their birthdays, but on the day of their death so as to signify a celebration of their entrance into the new life. Caroline Bynum writes, in *Fragmentation and Redemption,* that Christians happily returned to celebrate on such occasions in order to be with those who were "with God." Not fear, but attraction brought the community to the burial grounds, whether catacombs or cemeteries, because these bodies were now with Christ in glory. Just as we believe today, early Christians believed that the closest tangible proximity the living could have with Christ was in the Eucharist. Yet a Eucharist celebrated near the remains of one believed to be with God made it an even more intimate encounter with the body of Christ.

As Christianity grew within the empire and as its customs and prerogatives extended, churches were eventually built. At that time cemeteries gradually shifted position from beyond the city walls to surround the churches themselves. This occurred not simply because the church, where the Eucharist was celebrated, made the ground holy, but also because the bodies of the saints now in glory made the church's grounds holy.

RELICS AND THE RESURRECTION

We might pause for a moment to appreciate why the cult of relics has been so important for Catholics. Catholicism, in its appreciation of the sacramental, looks for the mediation of the presence of Jesus Christ. In that sacramental sense, relics (pieces of bone or hair or articles of clothing, for example) are important not for what they were, that is, a part of a once-living person, but rather for what they are: things that physically belonged to one who now is with God. For Christians, continuity between life on earth and life in heaven is mediated through the body.

DEACONS AND BURIAL RESPONSIBILITIES

While belief in the resurrection is, as Augustine notes, what separates Christians from all others, the Emperor Julian contended that one of the factors favoring the growth of Christianity was the great care Christians took in burying the dead. Though individuals often performed the task, the church as a community assigned it to the deacons, and, as Tertullian tells us, the expenses were assumed by the community. Lactantius reminds us further that not only did Christians bury the Christian dead, but they buried all of the abandoned: "We will not therefore allow the image and workmanship of God to lie as prey for beasts and birds, but we shall return it to the earth, whence it sprang: although we will fulfill this duty of kinsmen on an unknown man, humaneness will take over and fill the place of kinsmen who are lacking."

Eusebius too reports that during the plague that raged during the reign of Maximus, Christians cared for the sick and buried the dead. The Christian community accompanied the dead to their resting place, and their care for the dead extended not only to burying them but also to making offerings for the repose of their souls.

RESPECTING THE HUMAN BODY

The significance of burying the dead is then rooted in the profound respect that Christians have for the human body. The human body created and redeemed by God is to be raised up by God in glory. As such, then, it is the mark of the pledge of our deliverance. As a theologian, Cardinal

Walter Kasper has explained the importance of the human body for Christian theology:

> The body is God's creation and it always describes the whole of the human and not just a part. But this whole person is not conceived as a figure enclosed in itself, as in classical Greece, nor as a fleshy substance, as in materialism, nor as a person and personality, as in idealism. The body is the whole human in relationship to God and humanity. It is the human's place of meeting with God and humanity. The body is the possibility and the reality of communication.

As the "possibility of communication," to use Kasper's term, the human body, whether dead or alive, merits respect. But this, like the final kiss of the Christian corpse, is at times a very Christian claim. Nearly twenty years ago in *The Hastings Center Report* (1985), the liberal philosopher Joel Feinberg warned against the "trap of sentimentality" into which some might fall when giving any significant respect to dead bodies. But the Protestant ethicist William F. May responded in a way that recalls Kasper's words: "While living, a person identifies with his or her body in such a way as to render the dignity of the two inseparable. A person not only has a body, she is her body. . . . Yet while the body retains a recognizable form, even in death, it commands the respect of identity. No longer a human presence, it still reminds us of the presence that once was utterly inseparable from it." What Feinberg called sentimentality, we can call human insight illumined by faith.

POPULAR CULTURE AND CHRISTIAN BELIEFS

Popular culture typically evinces reverence for the dead human body because it expresses the continued presence of the person once known and loved. One of many recent examples of such reverence occurs in the brilliant movie *Last Orders,* based on the novel which won author Graham Swift the coveted Booker Prize. Referring to a brown urn poised atop a pub stool, David Hemmings asks Bob Hoskins apprehensively, "Is it Jack?" Hemmings, Hoskins, and two others are taking Jack's ashes to be cast off the shores of England to fulfill their wartime buddy Jack's final wishes. As they begin their day, they drink their draughts with Jack in the very pub where they had frequently met together on evenings for many, many years. As they set off on their daylong journey, they stop at a variety of war memorials and pubs, bringing Jack with them for each incursion. While sitting in the car they pass the urn from one to the other, giving each a turn to be a caretaker of Jack's remains. From dawn to dusk, until his ashes are scattered, Jack remains with them. We see just how present Jack is to his friends until his ashes are finally surrendered to the sea.

Even as ashes, the dead human body is still seen as the continued presence of the one we have lost. What differentiates the Christian understanding is that as Christians we believe that we each will be raised precisely in our human body. Small wonder at the care we take in accompanying through the centuries the bodies of the familiar and also of the abandoned as we lay them to rest.

• 8 •

Visit the Sick

$\mathscr{A}$lthough John's Gospel names the wedding feast at Cana as Jesus' first miracle, all three synoptic Gospels agree that healing the sick was Jesus' first miracle. Both Luke and Mark specifically name the healing of the demoniac as the first and the healing of Simon Peter's mother-in-law as the second (Mark 1:21–31; Luke 4:31–39). They, like Matthew (Matthew 4:23), note that the inauguration of Jesus' ministry was marked by many healings (Mark 1:32–34; Luke 4:40–41).

Like Jesus, his disciples attend to the needs of those whose health is in jeopardy. Mary's visit to Elizabeth is the first expression of Mary's own discipleship. She promptly responded to the Annunciation by attending to her cousin in need. Likewise, after the Pentecost, the disciples' ministry is marked by the physical and spiritual care of those in need. In turn, the twelve created the office of deacon to serve persons in need. It is important that we realize, for the most part, deacons and others did not attend to all people in need, but rather mostly those without family.

For two thousand years, the church has cared for the weak and the sick. A short overview shows just how important this work of mercy has been to the development of the church and its institutions.

THE PATRISTIC PERIOD

From the second to the fifth century, the bishop's deacon cared for the needs of five specific groups: foundlings, orphans, the aged, pilgrims, and the sick. Like the foundlings and orphans, the aged had no family to assist them. Similarly the sick were without family and were more likely new-comers, transients, or pilgrims. The deacons' care for pilgrims and the sick was a particularly onerous duty in pilgrimage centers. These centers of hospitality would eventually appropriately be called "hospitals."

Deacons became progressively associated with providing spiritual and physical support to the weak stranger. As their ministry developed, the church constructed appropriate institutions. The emperor Constantine, for instance, authorized every city to build and maintain facilities for the pilgrim, the sick, and the poor. As early as the fourth century, we have reports of hospitals. From the writings of St. Jerome we learn of a hospital in Rome; from St. Basil we hear about one he erected near Cappadocia. These institutions eventually divided labor, from which the separate practice of "nursing" emerged. The Christian community of Alexandria records five hundred nurses in AD 418 By the sixth century nearly all hospitals were under the administration of particular bishops.

THE MIDDLE AGES

Monasteries, too, began to construct medical facilities for infirmed pilgrims, many of which became centers for the study of medicine and for the production of medicinal herbs (readers of the *Brother Cadfael* mysteries by Ellis Peters should know that they are firmly rooted in history). The Hospitallers of St. Lazarus of Jerusalem, founded in 1120, was a military religious order. Sensitive to the fact that persons with contagious diseases were regularly excluded from hospitals, the Hospitallers operated hospitals for lepers, spread the faith, and protected pilgrims in the Holy Land. They also founded as many as three thousand *leprosaria* throughout Europe.

The motto of another group, the lay Order of the Holy Spirit founded by Guy de Montpellier, was: "The sick person is the head of the household; those who assist are the servants in the household." At its height, the order had founded and staffed in Europe some eight hundred hospitals. One of them, the Hospital of the Holy Spirit, still stands in Rome, a few hundred yards from St. Peter's Basilica.

In 1198, Pope Innocent III approved the Hospital of the Holy Spirit as the world's first apostolic hospital. Originally, it was erected to house pilgrims to St. Peter's Church, which was built on the site where Saints

Peter and Paul were martyred. Soon after the hospital was built, the order partitioned a section as a dormitory for the sick. When they realized that sick pilgrims, being strangers, might not know of their services, they searched the streets with carts (the forerunner of the modern ambulance) looking for the sick or stranded. Another part of the facility became a foundling hospital, allowing parents to abandon anonymously their babies to the care of the lay members. As these children grew, the order educated them in music—instruments and voice—so they could assuage the suffering of the sick, providing what we today refer to as "music therapy." The order also cultivated herbal and pharmaceutical resources and, as deaths occurred, developed laboratories for the study of the human anatomy through forensics.

As successful as such hospitals were, most historians refer to the work of the Eastern churches. In the early twelfth century, for example, the Monastery of Pantocrator in Constantinople operated simultaneously a hospital, a facility for persons suffering from mental illness, a pharmacy, a home for the aged, and a medical school.

Gradually, as European societies developed and their populations grew, the ministry of caring for the sick focused on particular types of diseases. In the thirteenth and fourteenth centuries, for instance, hospitals for the blind and the mentally ill begin to appear.

THE MODERN ERA

In the modern era, women religious have set the agenda for the care of the sick. The work of two religious orders provides an idea of their wisdom, commitment, and apostolic scope. What marks both orders is not only their care for those who are sick, but as importantly the incorporation of the sick into their homes and communities.

The Sisters of Charity of St. Vincent de Paul is a congregation of women founded by St. Vincent de Paul and Mademoiselle Le Gras. Their practices early on were considerably different from those of their contemporaries. While other women religious lived in convents, the Sisters of Charity of St. Vincent de Paul nursed the sick in their own homes, having (as the *Catholic Encyclopedia* notes) "no monastery but the homes of the sick, their cell a hired room, their chapel the parish church, their enclosure the streets of the city or wards of the hospital, having, as St.

Vincent says in the rule he finally gave them, no grate but the fear of God, no veil but holy modesty." Eventually the sisters were given hospitals to run and, later, the order constructed its own. It also established foundling homes, orphanages, and homes for the aged. Finally, going wherever the sick were to be found, some turned to nursing soldiers, winning the title "Angels of the Battlefield."

The Visitation Sisters (founded by St. Francis de Sales, Bishop of Geneva, and St. Jane de Chantal) welcomed the sick and weak into their own congregational life. They received into their order not only virgins but widows (on condition that they were legitimately freed from the care of their children), the aged (provided they were of right mind), the disabled (provided they were sound in mind and heart), and even the sick, except for those with contagious diseases.

TODAY

A look at health care in the United States today shows that about 13 percent of all beds belong to Catholic health-care institutions. The Catholic church is, therefore, the largest single health-care provider in the nation. Nearly all of these health-care centers were founded by women religious, whose distinct spiritualities grew into a legacy of care, adaptation, responsiveness, and inventiveness that is still active today. With diminishing numbers in their ranks, these religious orders are looking at a variety of ways of guaranteeing the future of their apostolic institutions while promoting their original charism. In a way they are handing on to another population the ministry that they have so ably led. Perhaps they are incorporating into their own original vision a partnership with others.

Consider the innovative Catholic Health Initiatives (CHI), whose stated mission is "to nurture the healing ministry of the Church by bringing it new life, energy, and viability in the 21st century. Fidelity to the Gospel urges us to emphasize human dignity and social justice as we move toward the creation of healthier communities." A national not-for-profit health-care organization, CHI is made up of sixty-three hospitals and forty-three long-term care, assisted and independent living, and residential facilities. Its ministry extends to ninteen states, serving sixty-four rural and urban communities, with more than sixty-seven thousand employees.

Multiple congregations entered into a partnership that, in turn, engaged lay leaders. CHI has formed a system that models the future of ministry in that it is a truly equal religious–lay partnership. Because of its commitment to promoting new models of health-care ministry, the hallmark of CHI is its mission and ministry fund. The fund assists projects described as "collaborative," "innovative," and "transferable" that address the root causes of illness in any of the communities they serve. Generating new offspring, CHI seeks to continue a ministry known for its inventiveness and responsiveness.

Today, too, many parishes are actively involved in visiting the sick through lay volunteers, the visits of extraordinary ministers of the Eucharist, and even the employment of professional nurses (see Mary Pat DeLambo's article on parish nursing, *Church,* Summer 2002). Since the moment Jesus first healed the sick, Christians have followed in his steps individually and collectively. With courage, compassion, wisdom, and imagination, the disciples of Christ today continue in that long-practiced work of mercy.

· 9 ·

Clothe the Naked

$\mathcal{G}$enesis 3:21 tells of the clothing of Adam and Eve by the Lord. It comes at a remarkable moment. Sin has led to punishment, but punishment is followed by gracious mercy. The sin of Adam and Eve leads not to death but to exile. And when Adam and Eve are sent into exile, they are protected by the Lord's merciful gesture of clothing them in the leather skins of wild beasts. Shortly afterward, the same cycle of sin and mercy occurs again with the murder of Abel by Cain. Cain is punished not by death but by exile, and he is similarly protected by the merciful marking of the Lord.

In the tenth book of *Paradise Lost,* John Milton describes this wonderful clothing of our first parents. His interpretation is remarkable: The one who clothes us in the garden is the one who disrobes himself at the Last Supper. In both actions, he assumes the position of a servant who dresses humanity and who later washes their feet as well. Milton writes:

> Then pitying how they stood
> Before him naked to the aire, that now
> Must suffer change,
> disdain'd not to begin
> Thenceforth the form of
> servant to assume,
> As when he wash'd his
> servants feet so now
> As Father of his Familie he clad
> Thir nakedness with Skins
> of Beasts

49

On several levels, Milton has caught an enormous scriptural claim. In the Old Testament, nakedness is always a sign of dependence. Two populations appear naked: babies dependent on their parents and prisoners of war dependent on their captors. Adam and Eve's sudden awareness of their nakedness represents, then, a newfound awareness of their dependence on the Lord. In response to their dependency, the Lord graciously dresses them.

Our "first parents" were to be clothed not only in the skin of beasts, but also in righteousness; that is, we are dependent on the Lord for our redemption. The Lord responds by assuming our humanity in order to redeem us. His incarnation also required him to assume our nakedness—both in the washing of the feet, as the Passion, and on the cross, as the Passion ends. The narratives of the Fall and redemption are written on the canvas of naked human bodies, both the sinners and the Savior.

I have always been struck by Milton's recognition that the clothing of Adam and Eve is the cause of Jesus' own nakedness at the Passion: He became naked for us who were and are naked. It was, of course, that very image that prompted many followers of the Lord to bare themselves: St. Francis would proclaim his absolute dependency on the Lord by baring his own flesh before his townspeople. In that gesture Francis wanted to illustrate his call to imitate the one who gave up everything, including his dignity, to respond to our dependency on him. Francis entered into solidarity with the One who entered into solidarity with us.

THE STORY OF ST. MARTIN OF TOURS

By entering into our nakedness, Christ entered into solidarity with us, both in the Garden of Eden and in the Passion. That solidarity is caught yet again in the famous story of St. Martin of Tours (316–397). I cite here the entire story from *The Life of St. Martin* as it was written by Martin's disciple, Sulpitius Severus (360–425). This is one of the first extended Christian texts, after the Scriptures, that was written to prompt emulation and imitation. The *Life* is one of the first biographical profiles of a saint whose own life was an imitation of Christ. In reading the story we may be surprised to see not the well-dressed Martin giving a part of his cloak (as El Greco and so many other famous painters have depicted him), but rather a nearly naked Martin sharing his last remaining bit of clothing. The story appears in the third chapter of the book:

> ACCORDINGLY, at a certain period, when he had nothing except his arms and his simple military dress, in the middle of winter, a winter which had shown itself more severe than ordinary, so that the extreme cold was proving fatal to many, he happened to meet at the gate of the city of Amiens a poor man destitute of clothing. He was entreating those that passed by to have compassion upon him, but all passed the wretched man without notice, when Martin, that man full of God, recognized that a being to whom others showed no pity, was, in that respect, left to him. Yet, what should he do? He had nothing except the cloak in which he was clad, for he had already parted with the rest of his garments for similar purposes. Taking, therefore, his sword with which he was girt, he divided his cloak into two equal parts, and gave one part to the poor man, while he again clothed himself with the remainder. Upon this, some of the bystanders laughed, because he was now an unsightly object, and stood out as but partly dressed. Many, however, who were of sounder understanding, groaned deeply because they themselves had done nothing similar. They especially felt this, because, being possessed of more than Martin, they could have clothed the poor man without reducing themselves to nakedness. In the following night, when Martin had resigned himself to sleep, he had a vision of Christ arrayed in that part of his cloak with which he had clothed the poor man. . . . After this vision the sainted man was not puffed up with human glory, but, acknowledging the goodness of God in what had been done, and being now of the age of twenty years, he hastened to receive baptism.

Martin's action was one of entering into the shame of the beggar. And in return Christ enters into the nakedness of the beggar so as to stand in solidarity with Martin.

PROVIDING CLOTHES TO THOSE IN NEED

Sensitivity to the dependence of others requires us not only to clothe the naked, but also those whose shame is associated with the quality of their clothing. Years ago I learned this lesson at the cost of another's embarrassment. In 1972, I worked doing outreach to migrant workers in different camps throughout upstate New York. I visited one camp regularly. Often I saw a boy playing in the dirt with his dog. Finally, I asked his mother why he wasn't in school. Her eyes cast down, she answered with acute shame, "He doesn't have the proper clothes."

To clothe those in need with dignity is something I learned in another context. For several months I lived in Edinburgh next to the beautiful St. Catharine's Convent of the Mercy Sisters. Several years ago, they entered into deliberations about electing a superior. One of the candidates, Sr. Aelred, to whom this book is dedicated, made it clear that were she elected the community would open its doors to the homeless. She was elected. After they began serving, several of the sisters recognized that many who came to eat needed to be able to shower and to get new clothing. What was once a kitchen, pantry, and dining room has extended to include showers, toilets, and changing facilities. Today the homeless project of the Mercy Centre serves up to about two hundred people a day with a rota of ninety volunteers.

As I learned from the Mercy Sisters of Edinburgh, clothing the naked has always meant recognizing the need to respond with dignity to those whose dependence on us is so evident. This is not a response of condescension. Rather, vesting them with new clothes is an attempt to bring them into ordinary familiarity and fellowship.

Around the world, the Society of St. Vincent de Paul is the lay association most easily associated with the task of clothing the naked. The society was originally formed in 1833 by six students in Paris; the group's founder, A. Frederic Ozanam (1813–1853), recognized the call to relieve need, but also to address the cause of the need. For this reason he identified two virtues for the society: the call of charity and of justice. Today, many recognize in his writings on social justice an anticipation of the social encyclical *Rerum novarum*.

Ozanam's society eventually expanded throughout the world. For instance, in 1845 a group of lay Catholics first met in St. Louis and formed the first council in the United States. The society has grown to the point where it now numbers some six hundred thousand members worldwide and has a presence in 132 countries.

We human beings find esteem in the way we look. By our appearance we see how we stand with others. When a person is most vulnerable, whether Adam and Eve or St. Martin's beggar, they need to be covered. The act of clothing the naked is an act of responding to the dependence of a fellow human being when they stand most in need.

II

A MEDITATION ON MERCY
IN LIGHT OF SEPTEMBER 11, 2001

• 10 •

Burying the Dead

$\mathcal{I}$ am sitting in Tübingen, Germany, on October 28, 2001, attending a small conference in this wonderful university town. We are seven moral theologians, invited to discuss the relationship between genetics and Roman Catholic theology. It is a real privilege to be here.

My dad died ten years ago today. I remember that week well, not so long ago. He had collapsed of a heart attack helping my brother, Sean, and his wife, Elisa, as they were cementing a walkway in front of their new home in Florida. He was only sixty-two years old.

A year before his death, Dad had to undergo emergency double-bypass surgery; he retired, then a fire erupted in their home, destroying everything my parents owned: their clothes, their furniture, their mementos, everything. Together they rebuilt that house, sold it, and moved to Florida. It was a hard ten months, living in noisy motels, waiting to move, when, my dad told me, "All I want to do is sit on the beach and hold your mother's hand."

Two months after they moved to Florida, while living in a rental, awaiting to take possession of their soon-to-be-built condominium, in all their expectancy and relief that the year was behind them, Dad collapsed. He had earlier told all of us that at his funeral he wanted one thing in particular: a bagpiper playing "Amazing Grace." As his body was carried out of our church the day of his burial, there stood the bagpiper, a fellow police officer, playing that song.

Later when we arrived at the cemetery on Long Island, my mom remarked that now my brother was no longer alone. Bobby had died in 1980. The second-born, Bobby came 360 days after I was born. He died twenty-six years later in a drowning accident. After his death, my parents had gone almost every Sunday to his grave. Now my dad would stay.

55

I am watching television in this efficient university guest house. I am constantly being told by the Germans here in Tübingen how they watched in horror on September 11. One of my companions, the German theologian Dietmar Mieth, remarks to another with us, the American theologian Lisa Sowle Cahill, that on that day he went to catch the television news at 3 P.M. (six hours ahead of Eastern Standard Time) as was his habit. He watched, astonished, as the second plane plunged into the second tower. He told us about sitting there stunned, receiving an e-mail minutes later from Lisa. When she hadn't mentioned the unspeakable tragedies in her e-mail, he realized that he in Germany knew then what she had not yet learned in Boston.

In Germany seven weeks after those events, I am watching the interdenominational service being held in New York to commemorate the dead at the World Trade Center. It is being carried "live." I realize that, like Dietmar, I am seeing this service before people living on the East Coast will see it.

Earlier in the day we had traveled to Würzburg, one of my favorite cities in Germany. We toured the archbishop's residence, an extraordinary Baroque palace, the greatest architectural work of that part of Germany. After climbing the magnificently frescoed staircase, we entered one more beautiful suite after another, finally passing through a long corridor showing photographs of the destruction of Würzburg in the last months of World War II. The entire city had been leveled—nothing but destruction. These beautiful rooms had been "restored." I thought of all the extraordinary achievement in these rooms and how they were brought to rubble.

Seeing that destruction, I immediately thought of another city. Last summer I volunteered to teach at Loyola School of Theology in Manila. One day, a friend took me for a walking tour of the old city. While strolling around, I found a statue of a woman holding her dead child, surrounded by other dead human bodies. It was a Filipino pietà commemorating the one hundred thousand Filipino citizens killed during the bombing raids from February 15 to March 15, 1945. Those strikes "liberated" that great nation, yet the tribute acknowledged that many of the bodies were never found, never buried. One hundred thousand persons killed in a month, in a war of liberation, many unburied.

As I looked at the photographs of Würzburg, another city "liberated" in 1945, I wondered where the unburied dead were.

Now, I am looking at the destruction of the World Trade Center. The interdenominational service hosts religious leaders on a stage framed by the wreckage, the remnants of the splendid girders of that incredible center. In the background, smoke rises from the ruins and water pumps hose these seven-week-old smoldering cauldrons. I am seeing rubble again, not unlike the rubble of Würzburg, not unlike the scenes of Manila I had imagined when looking at the pietà.

I remember the first time I went to the World Trade Center. I had been ordained in 1982. My family had hosted a wonderful first Mass reception for me, and after all the celebrations, before heading to Rome to do my doctorate, I invited them to a surprise dinner in New York City. My dad, sergeant detective of the Manhattan Homicide Squad, knew lower Manhattan like any cop or fireman. Yet, he could not figure out where our surprise evening would be. As we passed one restaurant after another that August evening, he kept anticipating the next as our destination. Even as I directed him into the parking lot of the garage under the WTC, my dad, "Kojak" as I called him, still had no idea where we were going. Neither did my mom, nor my brother; only my little sister. "I know where we are," gushed nineteen-year-old Jeannine.

That is when we first dined at Windows on the World, sitting by the windows, looking down on our great city in all its luminosity. When we learned that those wonderful windows framed by the girders were installed by a man named Keenan, it added to the magic.

We loved that restaurant and went there three other times: when I returned from Rome with my doctorate, when my brother proposed to his fiancée, and when my cousin graduated from the School of Visual Arts. It was our place for celebrations: the food, the service, the lights, the scenes, and the windows in their frames.

Now I sit in Germany looking at those very frames, smoldering.

As I watch this service, I think of the dead. I think of my dad and the way he loved the restaurant. I think of his younger colleagues, the NYPD officers who are now *buried, yet unburied* there in the rubble. I think of those from the Philippines, who were the waitstaff working the breakfast shift on that unforgettable morning in New York, *unburied, undocumented, unknown.* I listen to the sermons, wise words, consoling words, religious words, from Christians, Jews, and Muslims. Then Renée Fleming sings "Amazing Grace." That's when I begin to cry. Too many dead, too many buried, too many unburied.

I am moved beyond tears as I watch the mourners. One woman realizes that the television cameras are aimed at her and quickly hides her face. It is not modesty; she covers her face with a photograph. It's not her face, but her son's, David Graifin's, lost, unburied, in the rubble. *Unburied, but remembered,* by this photo that she wants us to see, even us here in Germany where I sit. She is burying him. Not a body, but an image, one we can all see, one whose name is broadcast on the picture for us all to remember.

Another mourner holds a portrait of Manuel Del Valle Jr., a firefighter; yet another holds a picture of Jason Coffey with his son, both lost in this unspeakable tragedy. All these photos hanging by hands held aloft, hundreds of portraits in a gallery as makeshift as the stage. *These people all are burying their dead.* We are the witnesses to their extraordinary actions of raising, filled with grief, their flesh and blood, their loving images of their beloved at the site of their deaths, where their mortal remains are beyond recognition. Even in Germany and elsewhere around the world, we can recognize them.

Earlier, the New York City mayor, in one of many magnificent gestures, gave these mourners an urn containing dirt from the rubble, a part of the burying ground, hallowed ground, an ashen mixture of animate and inanimate remains. He is helping them, us, bury the dead.

This great site of incredible power and elegance, of diversity and international commerce, is now a graveyard, without gravestones or markers, and it is *still* smoldering. There we see the hand of God burying the dead as we watch those firm hands raising their icons high.

Thinking on Würzburg, on Manila, on New York, on Dad, I hear the merciful words ". . . and grace will lead me home." I am somewhat consoled.

III

THE SPIRITUAL
WORKS OF MERCY

The Spiritual Works of Mercy

$\mathscr{L}$ike the corporal works of mercy, the spiritual works are seven: instruct the ignorant, counsel the doubtful, comfort the afflicted, admonish the sinner, forgive offenses, bear wrongs patiently, and pray for the living and the dead. While the corporal works call Christians to respond to those with specific needs that are lacking—shelter, food, water, clothing, and so on—the spiritual works are a little more complicated. On the one hand, like the corporal works, the first three deal with spiritual burdens that the neighbor suffers: the ignorant who lacks instruction in faith and morals, the doubtful who lacks the certitude of faith and morals, and the afflicted who experiences life's burdens not only corporally but also spiritually. The next three deal with matters of strife and reconciliation. They are appeals to the Christian to take significant steps toward maintaining the harmony of the community rife with many problems. In that sense the "spiritual" building-up is the reconciler herself, the one who admonishes, forgives, and bears wrongs. Certainly there is a spiritual building-up of the sinner, the forgiven, and the wrongdoer, but these three spiritual practices particularly redound to the reconciler and the community itself. By bearing wrongs patiently, the reconciler grows in virtue. Finally, the last spiritual work, the call to pray, builds up the entire community both through the one who prays and through the one for whom the practitioner prays.

While the beneficiary of the corporal works is the recipient, it is the reverse among the spiritual works: Often the beneficiary is the one who practices the spiritual works.

Unlike the corporal works, the spiritual works were first recommended to individuals. We saw a strong corporate legacy to each of the corporal works of mercy. Often an early diocese, a medieval religious order, a thirteenth-century lay association, or a Renaissance confraternity decided on a corporal task: ransoming the prisoner, sheltering the homeless, feeding the hungry. With the exception of the instruction of the ignorant, most of the spiritual works were not appropriated corporately but rather personally. There were no confraternities known for bearing wrongs patiently or forgiving offenses, however, nor were religious orders counseling the doubtful or admonishing sinners. Moreover, the calls to comfort the afflicted and pray for the living and the dead were so general that, unlike the corporal works, neither religious orders nor confraternities could assume them as specific charisms. Thus the spiritual works are proposed in a very general way to each and every Christian. They are not works looking for specific groups to assume them, but invitations to individual Christians to practice them.

Certainly, monasteries, religious orders, lay associations, and confraternities did practice these within their own communal identities. We can easily recall the famed chapter rooms, where individual monks knelt at the center of their communities and received the admonition of community members. But again, these were practices for the building-up of the individual and the community and were not charisms specific to a particular community the way the corporal works were.

LOOKING BACK TO
UNDERSTAND THE SPIRITUAL WORKS

The spiritual works developed in both Eastern and Western Christianity during patristic times. Origen recognized that Matthew 25 was not only a call to dress the body with clothes or to feed it with food, but also a summons to tend to the spiritual needs of the other. In many ways the roots of the call came through the appreciation of the Christian as being one—body and soul.

In the early literature the original corporal works had spiritual counterparts: the spiritually hungry, naked, thirsty, and so on. Moreover, inasmuch as Christians frequently sought to privilege the state of the soul over the state of the body, preachers from Origen through John Chrysostom warned listeners to attend not only to their siblings in need of physical nourishment, but also those in need of the word of God.

Such concerns were often accompanied by another set of issues. The epistles urged Christians to pardon, give mutual support, and exhort each other (as in Ephesians 4:32 and Colossians 3:13, 16). These biblical recommendations too were looking for a home in the emerging tradition of the church. Indeed, in 2 Corinthians 5, Paul urges his readers to become ambassadors of reconciliation, imitating the very action of God in reconciling the world. If the Christian is the follower of Christ the incarnate one, then the Christian is called to do what Christ did: reconcile.

This call to reconciliation, along with the call to be vigilant about the spiritual needs of the other, eventually coalesced into the spiritual works of mercy. The long-standing development through the tradition finds a comparable occurrence in the writings of Augustine. Around 378 in *De moribus ecclesiae catholicae,* Augustine describes a hodgepodge of concerns. But by 421, when he writes the *Enchiridion,* he proposes the corporal works of mercy and adds a few: console the afflicted, show the way to the lost, assist those who hesitate. Spiritual invitations to be mindful of other disciples on the way of the Lord are sensitive to the "weaker" sibling. They invite one to become the spiritual caregiver of others: building up oneself, one's weaker brother or sister, and the community as a whole. After proposing these three, Augustine offers a second form of "almsgiving": pardoning. In his sensitivity, Augustine sees the full picture, that pardoning is not only forgiving sins and bearing wrongs, but includes correcting and rebuking the sinner; this too is mercy (chapter 72).

Augustine then turns to the greatest of all alms: forgiving debtors and loving enemies. The one who has practiced the other works will be better able to realize this most challenging of all Christian tasks. For it is easy to do good to those who have done us no harm, but to forgive from the heart those who have harmed us is the real challenge of the Gospel. Augustine realizes that the challenge is fraught with difficulties and informs us that before we look to the great task of loving our enemy, we need to call on the Lord to have mercy on us. We need to recognize our own need for spiritual mercy. It is here, among the spiritual works of mercy, that we see Augustine's interest in promoting the love of self as he reminds the Christian to give alms first to her or his own self:

> For the one who wishes to give alms as he ought, should begin with himself, and give to himself first. For almsgiving is a work of mercy; and most truly is it said, "To have mercy on thy soul is pleasing to God." And for this end are we born again, that we should be pleasing

to God, who is justly displeased with that which we brought with us when we were born. This is our first alms, which we give to ourselves when, through the mercy of a pitying God, we find that we are ourselves wretched, and confess the justice of His judgment by which we are made wretched, of which the apostle says, "The judgment was by one to condemnation"; and praise the greatness of His love, of which the same preacher of grace says, "God commends God's love toward us, in that, while we were yet sinners, Christ died for us"; and thus judging truly of our own misery, and loving God with the love which He has Himself bestowed, we lead a holy and virtuous life. (chapter 76)

For Augustine, the works of mercy are very much a way for the Christian to acknowledge God's mercy. They bring the work of salvation full circle, helping the Christian to see the gift of mercy, which enables us to practice the task of mercy.

Finally, it is after Augustine that the seventh spiritual work, all-encompassing prayer for the living and the dead, emerges. Here, this third form of almsgiving, as it is named, is first conveyed as a general, but deeply felt well wishing for all people including one's enemies. The third form of spiritual almsgiving is a summary of all the foregoing.

LOOKING AHEAD

In *With All Our Heart and Mind: The Spiritual Works of Mercy in a Psychological Age,* Sidney Callahan reminds us of the "spirit" of the seven spiritual works of mercy. Each of them calls for a certain spiritual awareness, a certain in-depth, intuitive attentiveness to the needs of others. Recognizing a person as naked, imprisoned, or infirmed rarely requires a particular competency. But seeing one as afflicted, in doubt, reckless, or alienated requires a certain ready psychological sensitivity to the internal needs of one's neighbor. That learning to be attuned to the other is the real grace behind the spiritual works of mercy.

A Reconciling Spirit

KNOWING ONE'S NEED TO BE RECONCILED TO GOD

*A*dmonish the sinner, forgive offenses, and bear wrongs patiently—
these three spiritual works of mercy promote reconciliation. They are all
part of the one act of being a reconciling person, which is a key attribute for Christian discipleship. The foundation of being a reconciling
spirit lies in appreciating one's own need for reconciliation with God. As
Christians we cannot forgive, bear wrongs patiently, or admonish a sinner unless we understand ourselves as indebted to Christ, who perpetually offers *us* the way to be reconciled to God.

Nowhere is this clearer than in the Pauline summons (2 Corinthians 5) to be ambassadors of reconciliation. There Paul tells us that we are
no longer to regard anyone from the "human point of view." Rather, as
members of the new creation, we see that God in Christ has reconciled
us to himself and given us the ministry of reconciliation. Paul urges us
on behalf of Christ to be reconciled to God. Even though Paul notes that
Christ *has* reconciled us to God, still Paul urges us to be reconciled to
God. As any Christian recognizes, the need to be reconciled and the ac-
tual reconciliation take place throughout an entire lifetime. Note that
Paul's first concern is not that we be reconciled with one another (a
theme in 1 Corinthians), but rather that we be reconciled *to God*.

Centuries later, Thomas Aquinas develops the same insight when
writing on the topic of fraternal correction in the context of the practices of mercy. Thomas asks whether the act of admonishing one's
brother or sister in Christ is itself an act of mercy or an act of justice. If
we admonish someone because of the harm they bring to another,

Thomas says, then it is an act of justice because we are concerned with the victim, the one who ought not to be so treated. But, if we admonish the sinner because by sinning the sinner is out of union with God, then the admonition is an act of mercy. Worried about that person's need for union with God, we admonish them.

A PRESUMPTUOUS GENERATION

Today it is hard for us to realize just how much we need to be reconciled to God because we live in a presumptuous age. From Augustine and Aquinas we know that all virtues have two contrary vices. Hope, for example, has the two contrary vices of despair and presumption. Where former generations erred in their despair, ours errs in its presumption.

In previous generations, the church often informed us of our sinfulness. We heard frequently the phrase *massa damnata,* that incredible, despairing insight from the early medieval church, which held that most people were damned to hell. During the 1950s and 1960s, however, we began to look on the breadth of the mercy of God and to see the frequency with which the Scriptures pointed to the offer of salvation as extended to all people. We started, rightly I think, to repudiate the despairing notion of *massa damnata* and focused instead on our hope in God's mercy.

Perhaps a generation later, however, we have moved from the universal offer of God's mercy to the universal claim of humanity's goodness. Certainly, there is a goodness that we rightly assert as having been created in the image of God. Yet there remains a presumption about how pervasive our goodness is. If we are so good, one wonders why Christ died, why there is the cross, whether we really need God's mercy. Many writers have tried to explain why people today seem not to need (or are not aware of their need for) the sacrament of reconciliation. My explanation is simple: Ours is a presumptuous generation.

We have come full term in a self-serving circle. From the despairing belief that the majority of persons are going to hell (a self-serving belief since many who preached it believed that everyone else was damned), we have moved to the equally self-serving belief that we all merit salvation because we are so good. Anyone who spends but a jot of time considering the sorry state of our moral lives, however, recognizes the pervasiveness of sin (in our pettiness and jealousies), the limits of the human condition, and the profound need we all have for the cross and redemption of Christ.

While I myself believe in the universal offer of salvation, I am frightened by the parable about the wedding guest who didn't even bother to put on the wedding garment provided him. In that parable (Matthew 22:2–14) we recognize the sin of presumption. It also appears in the parable of the unforgiving steward (Matthew 18:23–35). Because of such presumption, I recognize my need for reconciliation as I ask God's mercy on me, a great sinner.

Being reconciled with God requires a recognition of our own sinfulness. For myself, I find that as I live out my priesthood, my sinfulness and my need to be reconciled to God become ever more apparent to me. Whenever I preside at a liturgy, I am more and more deeply aware of what an unworthy priest I am. As I begin the liturgy by kissing the altar, I offer up my unworthiness to God in that action. I let go to God all my sinfulness; I kiss the altar not only to reverence it but to leave my brokenness and my sinfulness there and to surrender to God's call, God's vocation. It is a humbling and liberating ascetical practice of recognizing my own indebtedness to God. The presider's action moves into the liturgy as it opens with the sign of the cross and the Kyrie (Lord, have mercy), the ever present, ever repetitive recognition of Paul's urgent summons.

Like my students, perhaps you as a reader are surprised by my darkness. I think of sin as the failure to bother to love. Given that definition, I think we sin a lot more than we realize. Inasmuch as evil is especially deceptive, the ability to see one's sinfulness is not easy, nor can it be taken for granted. The great late German moral theologian and rector of the University of Bonn, Franz Böckle, noted that we do not know our sinfulness until we begin to acknowledge it; then the act of confessing allows us to see the depth of our sinfulness. The "catch-22" of presumption is that the presumptuous never know how presumptuous they are.

Though they find it a bit jarring, I do not hesitate to tell my students that we are worse than we think we are. Years ago, I was shaken by this insight while taking a course with Fr. John O'Malley, S.J., and reading Martin Luther. Luther never tired of telling his listeners how bad they were. In my presumptuous years, I asked O'Malley why they bothered to listen to Luther. "Because he spoke the truth," O'Malley said.

PRACTICING THE THREE WORKS

Knowing ourselves as sinners prompts us to forgive one another. This action, the synoptic Gospels make perfectly clear, is also a lifelong process. Since we are constantly in need of being reconciled to God, we are constantly in need of being reconciled with one another. How many times? Jesus was asked. Seventy times seven times.

The possibility of Christianity depends on reconciliation. Nowhere, not even in Antioch, could people have seen the love Christians had for one another were it not for the regular practice of reconciliation. No Christian marriage, no Christian community, no Christian apostolate, no Christian parish or diocese can exist without reconciliation. Reconciliation makes it all possible. Knowing oneself as a sinner becomes the condition that keeps (or should keep) us Christians from assuming an arrogant stance as we admonish the sinner, forgive trespasses, and endure wrongs. Rather than assuming an air of moral superiority in any of these practices, we need only be reminded of Paul's urging to be reconciled to God; the Christian pillar of moral superiority is made out of sand.

Today we see both presumption and the need for reconciliation in the present crisis over leadership and sexual abuse. We still need to admonish those who engage in scapegoating or who try to avoid the responsibility to promote a stronger culture of accountability and integrity. Yet we must do this in straightforward, humble ways, concerned for both the sinners and those whom they harm.

We also need to forgive. We do that by recognizing when we have sufficiently brought wrongdoing to light. As the famous Truth and Reconciliation Commission in South Africa taught us, we must reveal adequately the wrongdoing so as to be able to forgive. We cannot forgive without an acknowledgment of the wrongdoing. We cannot be silent about wrongs, something we have learned, I hope, from the cover-ups of the scandal itself. But as the revelations become complete, the accountability acknowledged, and the restitution accomplished, we must forgive.

Finally, we need to bear harms patiently. Here we must discern well who is called to practice this spiritual work: Too often, abused wives, like abused children and others, were told to bear harms patiently. Rather, we must be vigilant about the way this spiritual work has endangered and, in some instances, destroyed the body and spirit of the very vulnerable.

We must also note those Christians who in their confidence in Christ bear harms patiently.

I think of two wonderful people connected with the founding of the Common Ground Project: Monsignor Philip J. Murnion and Cardinal Joseph Bernardin. As they attempted to forge a more reconciled church, a variety of persons attacked and tarnished the integrity of the proponents and their project. In response, rather than condescend into scandalous discourse, they took the high road. Bearing those harms patiently, they became models of what Paul meant for us to do in similar situations.

· 13 ·

Being Vigilant

$\mathscr{T}$he three spiritual works of mercy—instructing the ignorant, counseling the doubtful, and comforting the afflicted—are practices that train us to look elsewhere. They call us to a new vigilance, a new vision, and a new sympathy. This call stands out loud and clear against other messages we hear today.

Though there is no doubt that human sympathy is valued by contemporary culture, the industrialized urban world really does not want us to linger too long or focus too much on persons whose lot is worse than our own. We sense a certain discomfort when faced with a depiction of the human condition as being less than we would like it to be. Like surfing the television and coming to a news segment on famine, if we linger too long, invariably somebody will ask us to "turn the channel, please."

In a manner of speaking, members of contemporary society worry about where we turn our eyes. Think, for instance, of university offices that give very specific directions to prospective students about how to enter the campus for a recruitment visit. The campus might be bordered on two sides by state-subsidized housing, the other two sides by beautiful parks. Even if the quicker route runs through the poor neighborhood, the carefully designed directions tend to take the recruits (and their tuition-paying parents) through the longer scenic route.

Like most societies, ours has a certain self-promoting tone. We do not want to suggest that our society is anything less than we want it to be. We do not like facing wherever our failures lie, preferring to look to our destiny as we imagine it to be. This is not simply an American tendency; it is a global one. Twelve years ago, while on an immersion experience of China with professors from six different U.S. seminaries, a bureaucrat in Beijing told us that there were only a dozen or so homeless persons in Beijing. He assured us that we would never see a homeless person. Five minutes after leaving his office, however, we saw a young adolescent sleeping on the streets. "He must be one of the unseen dozen," my colleague remarked.

Of course, we saw that young man by looking downward in a city that, like all modern cities, invites us constantly to look upward. We look up to see whether we can cross a street, to appreciate a landmark, to gaze at a skyline, or to look at a billboard. We avoid those in need on the street as we inevitably look elsewhere.

WHAT ATTRACTS OUR GAZE?

The father of modern-day capitalism appreciated the importance of looking upward. Adam Smith, author of *The Wealth of Nations,* wrote another work, *The Theory of Moral Sentiments*, about the type of virtues a modern-day capitalism ought to develop. Among the virtues that Smith proposed was sympathy or fellow feeling. The object of sympathy, Smith argued, ought to be the wealthy, industrious leader. We ought to establish a sense of being connected with and in favor of the financially successful businessperson, wrote Smith.

It sounds odd at first glance. Why be sympathetic to someone who has prestige, wealth, and fame? Still, Adam Smith was an astute student of human nature. As a matter of fact, most people are emotionally disposed to the successful. That disposition is the very wellspring upon which advertisers around the world depend. Most of what is dangled before us to purchase and consume is recommended precisely by the people we want to see, meet, and be like.

In a manner of speaking, Smith realized that you and I are "hardwired" to be attracted to the successful. People who want to sell us anything—an education, a university, a garment—know that the best way of attracting our attention is to place their product beside attractive people. Our eyes naturally look up to them.

PRACTICES THAT FOCUS OUR ATTENTION RIGHTLY

By contrast, nowhere is the call to look elsewhere more evident than in the story of the rich man and Lazarus. Ironically, the rich man was unable to see the poor man who sat on his very doorstep. The text plays on our sense of position when, after his death the rich man cries up from Hades to Abraham. The one who once could not bother to look down is now so far down himself that he can only look upward, in longing, for all eternity.

This and other frightening admonitions from the Gospels prompt us Christians to see that we are called to be vigilant about the needs of our neighbor. Unlike the priest and the Levite who were unable to see the wounded man on the road to Jericho, we are called to develop a new sense of expectation, *a sense of being ready for someone else's difficulties.*

For this reason, the Gospels train us to see whether—in regard to those on the road—we are willing to define ourselves as their neighbors. Are "our neighbors" merely those who can return whatever favors we give them? The Gospels admonish us against associating only with those who are our equals, whether in intelligence, prosperity, health, or confidence. Rather, we are to include persons who are excluded, marginalized, and overlooked by society.

The tradition offers three specific practices to train us in such vigilance and sympathy, responsive corollaries to those who suffer the loss of the three theological virtues: faith, hope, and charity.

1. Instruct the Ignorant

Tradition considers instructing the ignorant as ministering to those who need better education in the faith. Catechetical programs are designed specifically to answer this need. Since Jesus first preached the Good News, he has taught us to seek those who would be most comforted by it. All our religious education programs—for adults, young adults, and children—are premised on the need to instruct the people so that they may be fully incorporated into the community of faith.

2. Counsel the Doubtful

Counseling the doubtful has also meant being aware of the needs of persons uncertain about matters of hope. When I preside at funerals, for example, I see, very broadly speaking, two types of people mourning the beloved. First, some of the mourners are persons who are no longer or never were believers in God and God's promises. For them the funeral is a defining moment of farewell. They now hope to keep the beloved alive in their hearts and minds. Other mourners, though, are Christians caught in the ambiguous time of living between the already and the not yet. Already we are saved, but we do not yet live in the state of glory. Some of these people hope in the resurrection but are caught in the waiting experience where doubt, too, arises.

I have always found that counseling the doubtful requires sensitive honesty. On the one hand, one must recognize the legitimacy of doubt, while, on the other, also affirming the hope we all share. Counseling the doubtful requires not lessons of instruction so much as the personal communication of one another's experience of the rightfulness of Christian hope.

3. Comfort the Afflicted

Comforting the afflicted is a response in charity to the neighbor who is suffering. More specifically, it is an act of mercy, of entering into the chaos of another so as to respond to the person in need. The afflicted are always those who have suffered loss, whether of a basic human capability (for instance, losing one's hearing) or of a basic relationship (losing one's parent or spouse). Affliction comes from loss. Comforting the afflicted is not, however, an attempt to compensate or replace the loss. Rather, the Christian who stands in love with the one who suffers is a faithful friend and a witness to the other.

Comforting is always an act of acknowledging, not so much the loss, but the self-understanding of the afflicted one. To comfort means to respond with an *active listening* to the one who wants to express her or his affliction.

A FINAL WARNING ABOUT
LOOKING AT PERSONS IN NEED

Because Christians dare to look elsewhere, because they become vigilant of the "omnipresent Lazarus," they could begin to assume a stance of condescension toward those to whom they seek to respond. Mistakenly, a Christian could treat the "ignorant" adult as a child instead of an adult; "the doubtful" as despairing or neurotic instead of as spiritually honest and searching; "the afflicted" as unable to articulate or respond to their own sense of loss. In short, in each instance, the Christian could try to "take charge" of the neighbor's life and thereby treat the neighbor as an *object* of mercy rather than as a person in need. Christians, because they look elsewhere, might begin to look down on those to whom they minister. This may not be surprising, but it is never acceptable.

MINISTRY IS SERVICE

A helpful corrective to my own initial tendency to condescend is to recognize that my ministry ought to be a form of service. When I assume the position of servant to the ignorant, the doubtful, and the afflicted, I lose (unfortunately not often enough) my own sense of superiority, which is always an obstacle to being neighborly. Behind this corrective is a final appreciation of real Christian vigilance. These three spiritual works of mercy teach us to be vigilant. By participating in the life of mercy, we may discover the dignity of the human person that sparkles oftentimes when they are most vulnerable. That is a lesson we are invited to learn our whole lives long.

· *14* ·

Prayer

$\mathcal{R}$ecently, I called my mother in Florida. "Hey, I couldn't find you at all yesterday. Where were you?" "I was with your brother. He's in the hospital." My brother Sean is forty-one years of age, lives in West Boca Raton in Florida with his wife and two young sons. He has had health problems before. Last year, on the eve of undergoing emergency back surgery, he had a pulmonary embolism. "What is it this time?"

Sean was in terrible pain with blood in his urine and legs terribly swollen that left him immobile. For the next two weeks he stayed in a community hospital where his doctor ran all sorts of tests and tried to determine the underlying problem.

In the meantime, I had a lecture in Chicago and then I had to host a small conference in Leuven, Belgium. I talked with Sean daily; he was in constant agony. As I was heading off to Belgium, I spoke with Sean's doctor. He was checking to see if Sean had cancer. I called my sister-in-law, Elisa, to suggest that her brother, Michael, a physician, should talk with Sean's doctor just to get a sense of whether the doctor really knew what he was going after.

I went to Belgium, but couldn't sleep my entire time there. In fact, just as the conference began, I went to the emergency room for an allergic (stress related?) reaction. Should I not be with my brother, I kept thinking.

In the meantime Elisa talked with Michael and her cousin Stephen (another doctor, in his case a hematologist), and both came to the conclusion that Sean had another major clot and that he needed to be transferred immediately to a major health–care facility, but where would they get an admitting physician? Stephen, a fellow at Miami's Jackson Memorial, assured Sean and Elisa that he would work on it. Upon returning from Belgium, I flew to Florida to be with Sean, but because of a variety of other commitments I could only be there for twenty-four hours. Sean was waiting to be transferred. Michael and Stephen were absolutely right; Sean had an enormous clot in his inferior vena cava and needed to have a fairly complicated, extensive, emergency procedure.

Sean was transferred late that night and by the time I arrived back in Boston he was undergoing the three-day-long procedure. Stephen oversaw everything. Stephen saved my brother's life, but Stephen said it was a miracle that he managed to get Sean in time.

I write this today, Thanksgiving eve; we expected that Sean would be going home but they found two more clots in his legs.

PRAYER

During these past six weeks, I have been praying a lot. When I was not talking (from a distance) with Sean, Elisa, my nephews, and my mom, all I could do was pray. Going to bed at night or arising in the middle of the night or the early morning with plenty of anxieties, all I could do was turn to God with my need. I learned a lot about prayer, the prayer of supplication, the practice that is the seventh and final work of mercy.

I found that there were three main dimensions to my prayer: the search for a specific answer, being united with my brother, and being transformed by prayer. Let me say something about each.

Effective Prayer

First, and above all, I wanted my prayer of supplication to be effective. Keep Sean well, deliver him from his agony, find out his problem, get him into Jackson, help him through the procedure. My prayers were specific and my expectations were as well. Be with him, Lord, do not let him falter, comfort him in his hospital loneliness and suffering.

I do not have a theology of how God responds directly to suffering, nor do I have a theology of God's direct interference into the ordinary life of the world. But I knew, on my knees, that I wanted the One who healed so many to be with my brother and his physicians and nurses throughout the ordeal. I wanted God to hear my prayers and see to my brother's life.

I am a firm believer in saying exactly what I want in prayer. No mincing on the desires, I believe in plain speaking. I do not go for the pious strategy of saying, "whatever you will, God." I'm like Abraham: I beg, argue, plea, even if necessary, bargain. I figure, God will do what God wants to do; in the meantime, I want to be sure that God hears exactly what I want.

I have had enough loss: Besides my family home being destroyed in a fire, I lost my other brother (Bob), my father, and my niece, Megan. With my sister, brother-in-law, nephew, and Megan herself we fought long and hard for Megan's health, and we begged and pleaded. And even though we lost Megan, I still prayed as hard for Sean this time. I could not do otherwise.

When we pray for specific results we can actually feel the energy of our hopes and desires being expressed. I know that firsthand. I know how much of myself I brought to this prayer these past few weeks. But I know of other instances when I have felt the power of others' prayers.

For instance, I remember on several occasions entering a church where people had prayed, and I literally sensed the power of their prayer. Living in Italy as I did for my doctoral studies, I remember the first time I entered the crypt in the Basilica of Assisi to pray at the tomb of St. Francis and had a physical awareness of the centuries of fervor prayed before the tomb of Francis. I could feel the prayers that had been uttered there. I found the same elsewhere, like the tomb of St. Anthony of Padua, where with millions of other pilgrims I placed my hand on the saint's tomb and felt the energy of hope and desperation.

It is not, of course, a private feeling. I remember being at the pilgrim church at Chimayo and having the same feeling; I watched people as they entered the simple church, immediately going on their knees upon entering the church. They felt or knew viscerally that they were in a place where Christians prayed fervently for centuries.

Unitive Prayer

These specific expressions of hope and pleading move me to the second dimension of prayer, that is, the unitive. In Chicago, Boston, and Leuven, away from my brother, I felt closer to him in prayer than I did when I spoke to him by phone. In my prayer to Christ, I found that Christ helped me to be with my brother. Bringing Sean to Christ, Christ brought Sean to me. It was as if in my prayer Christ gave me a sacred place to be with my brother. While I could do nothing but pray, I found that in my prayer I drew closer to him in his suffering.

I think this unitive dimension of prayer is fairly common. By prayer we draw close to the ones whose concerns we bring to Christ. And Christ brings us in turn to the ones for whom we pray. This is why the prayer of the faithful is so important in the liturgy, because by it not only does the community become more mindful of the needs of others, but they are brought in turn by Christ to the community, into the Eucharistic celebration. By our prayer, we are united to those for whom we pray; they enter into our communion.

In my anxiety for my brother and in my distance from him, I found myself in prayer feeling close to him in a way I could not otherwise attain. And I found peace there in that sacred space that Christ granted me. It was as if the space was an oasis of tranquility.

Transformative Prayer

Finally, there is the transformative dimension of prayer. Like all the spiritual and corporal works of mercy, we become transformed by the practice of mercy. Christ transforms both those whom we raise up and ourselves. By being merciful we enter as Christ did into the world of another's suffering and we become transformed by their suffering, by our encounter with them, and by the presence of Christ who hears and responds to us in our need. By entering into another's chaos we are affected and shaped both by our loved one and by Christ. By this mercy we encounter a hope that we are not afraid to have.

We are touched and transformed in that hopeful, tranquil space where Christ lets us be united with the loved one. In that space, we find that despite our anxieties, we are able to stand, beg, and hope. Confronting our greatest fears and deepest desires, we encounter in our prayer the most important concerns and people in our lives. In that hope-filled space, Christ lets us face these fears and these desires, these concerns and these people, as we face him. There in that sacred space we find ourselves able to face what we so often miss, the love that holds our lives together.

Tomorrow I will call Sean and Elisa, my nephews and my mom. I will wish them a Happy Thanksgiving and tell them how much I love them. I will also call Stephen to thank him for saving my brother's life. But before all else, I will look for Christ and that sacred space where I found a peace, and I will bring to him again my prayers for my brother, Sean.

IV

A MEDITATION ON PRIESTHOOD IN LIGHT OF THE CHURCH'S SCANDALS

· 15 ·

Being a Minister of Mercy

$\mathcal{O}$ver the past four years I have been writing a column in *Church* magazine about mercy and its willingness to enter into the chaos of another. But during the past two years in Boston, I have come to learn a great deal about what it means to be a priest today. In my experience, I find that as I enter into other people's chaos, I also enter into my own, which teaches me just how limited I am. I used to think that that insight was a curse. I realize now it is a blessing. For that reason, I want to share with you what one needs to be a minister of mercy. Foremost among these needs is the humility that comes of self-knowledge.

Let me tell you how I started my presentation last month to a group of sixteen Jesuits who would be ordained the following week to the diaconate as a final stage of their preparation for priestly ordination.

"I am not a well-ordered person. Seriously. I don't say that to make anyone impressed with my humility. I know myself and as I stand before God, the only thing I can think of is my gratitude for the mercy of Christ's death and resurrection which he accomplished for me."

I tried to tell them that I am mature, I am responsible, but inside of me the pieces do not come together as well as I would like. As Walt Whitman wrote in "Song of Myself," "I contain multitudes." That's me to a tee. I write on virtues and recognize the claim of the "unity of the virtues," but that claim is far off on the horizon of my expectations. I am pulled in a variety of directions, daily.

I bring my multitudes into my prayer. When I preside at the 5 P.M. Sunday liturgy at St. Peter's in Cambridge, I process down the aisle, singing the entrance song with the choir and congregation. When I get to the altar, I reverence it with a kiss and I pause and say, "I hand myself completely over to you." I learned this after many years of pausing, kissing the altar, and thinking to myself, "What am I doing here. I have no business being here." Now I simply let go in prayer.

Despite all our protestations, none of us live transparent lives and I, with my multitudes, am amazed at where I am now. I am a priest, in Boston no less, writing about ethics.

A GREAT TIME TO BE A PRIEST

"Tell them it's a great time to be a priest. Never has the church needed priests more; never has the call to priesthood been more important." This is what my friend and colleague Cathy Mooney, a lay theologian, said recently at a faculty council meeting when someone asked our superior how the guys who were going to be ordained to the diaconate were faring. "Ambiguous," he answered. "It's understandable." To that, Cathy uttered her prophetic words.

I agree. I have never been more affirmed in my priesthood than in this past year. More laypeople write me notes, e-mails, or stop after the liturgy to thank me for my priesthood, presiding, and preaching. As hard as these days have been, as poor as the church has appeared, as incredible as our faith must seem, I have never felt that my vocation was more important.

In early February 2002, a week after news of Father Geoghan first appeared in the *Boston Globe,* one parishioner said to me after the liturgy, "The sermon was good, but aren't you going to comment on the crisis?" I thought, "In a homily?" But then I took it to heart. And I started the next week. I applied the Gospel to the chaos here in Boston. I found the Gospel come alive and my vocation as well.

More is at stake now. Like everywhere else, some Catholics no longer come to church. Many who remain are looking for reasons to stay. So I worry. I worry about what to say and then how to say it. I worry about those who want to hear something and about those who cannot stand hearing any more about it. I worry whether I am fair, whether I am too political, whether I am speaking clearly, whether I am cheapening the Gospel.

I have never taken my priesthood or my preaching more seriously though, and so I pray during the liturgy. I pray as I did during my own ordination when, lying prostrate, the multitudes were really working overtime, reminding me that I had no business being here. Now as I listen to the readings, as I sing with the congregation the responsorial psalm, I go over my sermon, hoping that I will bring the Gospel to bear. After I preach, I feel no real relief. But it is over and I let go again. I think of my prayer at reverencing the altar.

THE BOSTON PRIESTS' FORUM

In the spring of 2002 I started going to the monthly meetings of the Priests' Forum of Boston. At my first meeting, a man who had been molested by a priest told his tale—for two hours. He was there at the priests' invitation. They recognized that they needed to listen, needed to hear and learn what was so tragic in the events of this crisis. What an introduction! Here I was after eleven years of living in Boston, and this was the first time I was meeting with my brother priests. What an identity we shared!

Whenever I arrive at the monthly priests' forum meeting, I find about two hundred, mostly diocesan priests getting ready for the gathering. Almost to a man, the priests come up to me and say, "Thank you for coming." They are in the trenches, but they thank me because I am a religious order priest and I am identifying with them. Of course, I learn from them—in their simple welcome, in their fraternity, in their profound modesty—more about my priesthood. I hear how they have heard the laity ask, "Are you going to say anything about the crisis?" I see how they have answered. I hear how they defend these new lay movements like Voice of the Faithful. And in this whole mess, many of us priests have learned from them how we should proceed.

LEADERSHIP, MODESTY, POWER

As the year progressed I began to see my nation prepare for war with Iraq. Ethically I could not find grounds for such a war. I wonder where moral leadership is today. In both the church and in my nation, I feel leaderless. Nor do I think that the promises of tomorrow are all that appealing. On the contrary, I think that darkness looms on the horizon precisely as I watch our leaders, confident, with clear firm messages, assuring us.

Still I have hope. I have hope when I meet with my modest friends at the priests' forum. I have hope when I hear a priest like Walter Cuenin speak to reporters and convey the concerns of his parishioners. I have hope when I hear Mary Jo Bane, a political scientist at Harvard, or Stephen Pope, a moral theologian at Boston College, commenting on the need for honesty, accountability, and integrity, as well as more inclusive ways of proceeding in leadership. I have hope when I see our deacons asking us during the liturgy of ordination to get on our knees and pray for them as they, in their ambiguity, lie prostrate. I have hope as I see my graduate assistant, Colleen Vogt, work to start a local chapter of Voice of the Faithful.

In all of these movements I find that, like me, the participants have a modesty. They do not follow the old models of leadership, projecting confidence, drawing clear lines, assuring us of the rightness and firmness of their ways. The people I am admiring these days are *much more modest,* much more honest about their apprehensions. They have the same ambiguities, the same sense that they may be wrong on this point or that. They have the same limited, human self-understanding that I do as I wonder and doubt my own adequacy about how I am proceeding.

I think the reason I find hope today—in my friends around the city or in the priesthood that I too live and share—is that when I enter into my own chaos or theirs, or into the chaos of the church or of the nation, I no longer appropriate an *infallible persona.* I have learned how limited I am. I have hope in myself and in them as real persons, limited but real.

Perhaps that other type of leader would say that that is a luxury they cannot afford. I do not agree. One deacon wrote me a note after his ordination. By talking about my own infirmities, I let him imagine himself as priest in the person he really is and not some construct. I gave him a reason to be courageous about himself, a courage that my friend Donald Cozzens constantly urges us priests to embrace.

I learned to acknowledge my limitedness the hard way. I could refer to a couple of learning lessons, but one will do. I was about to give a new lecture in my introductory course to moral theology at Weston Jesuit. The new lecture was about spirituality and morality. One student had already expressed on several occasions her doubt about the correctness of my teaching. Before I began this lecture, which was designed to be, I thought, well beyond even my own expectations, she raised her hand and criticized me for something from the last class. I lost it and in two minutes I verbally "put her in her place." Then I began the lecture on spirituality being completely assured of myself and the power I had and the order I had restored.

ADMITTING WRONG

I did not sleep that night. It seemed all so stupidly incongruous. I let a querulous student get the better of me. Worse, I did not appreciate the enormous difference of power we held, she and I. Worse still, in a course on ethics for ministry I completely lorded my power over a student. I began the next class with an explanation. I said that I had been taken off guard, that I had overused my power, that by my own bombast I had tried to intimidate a student. I then acknowledged before all fifty graduate students my own exasperation that this one student never let me get to first base, yet that did not warrant, in any way, my response. Finally, I said I was wrong and that I was sorry, to the student and to the class. My explanation gave a context to everything; my apology—a very different action—was an acceptance of my own responsibility.

I remember as I apologized that I thought, they will never have reason to believe in me again. But as a matter of fact, I was no longer the expected, the predictable, the projected. Instead, I became in their eyes more real, more human, and therefore *more authoritative* than I had been before. I had learned in that class a lesson about myself, about power, and about humanity.

In light of the way our nation has responded to attacks on us and in light of the way our church has responded to the crisis of clergy sexual abuse, I wonder what we are learning about power. In quiet ways, here in Boston, I have learned that being a priest is realizing that even at this time and in this city, I have a great deal of power. More importantly, I see that such power depends very much on my acceptance of my own fallible humanity.

V

MERCY AND THE
EUCHARISTIC LITURGY

· *16* ·

The Entrance Rite

$\mathcal{V}$irtue ethics reminds us that we become what we do. Wherever we are, we are shaping ourselves by the practices that we engage as parents, ministers, laborers, writers, students, businesspeople. We become the agenda that we set.

Likewise, the church forms itself by the practices it promotes. To the extent that the church practices mercy, we become—in some measure— merciful. To the extent that it stands intolerant, we become intolerant. In the same way, a parish becomes hospitable by practicing hospitality. What we do as church shapes us as church.

In a book that I edited with the Mennonite theologian Joseph J. Kotva Jr., *Practice What You Preach: Virtues, Ethics, and Power in the Lives of Pastoral Ministers and Their Congregations,* twenty-five Christian ethicists from around the country asked how is it that church practices affect the type of people we become. In each of four sections we entertained questions about the way our pastors are formed, the way they live their lives, the way congregations are formed, and the way they behave. In each essay, the specific author proposed a way that the church proceeds and asks, "But is it ethical?"

This is, in some sense, a new question. When we ask questions about how the church proceeds, for example, regarding lay leadership, promoting pastors, or arbitrating doctrinal conflict, we usually look to canon law, theological assertions, and ecclesiological practices. But we seldom include among those inquiries, ethics. We don't ask, "But is it ethical?"

Similarly, when we Roman Catholics look at the way we ought to worship, we appeal to canon law, church teaching, and liturgical norms,

91

but we hardly ever ask, "What is the ethical way of worshiping?" Other churches, however, do ask that question. The Greek Orthodox theologian Joseph Woodill writes in *The Fellowship of Life: Virtue Ethics and Orthodox Christianity* that liturgy is where we become illuminated about how we are to be conformed to God. Liturgy is where we understand ourselves as the people we are called to become: In liturgy we Christians stand in community before God as a people saved and called to be sanctified.

LITURGY AND VIRTUE

Liturgical practices shape us for today and forever. If we were to look back at the last century, unquestionably we would see that the most significant event for the Roman Catholic Church has been the reform of the liturgy. Noteworthy events occurred throughout the century, including the writing of the social encyclicals; the papacies of Popes Pius XII, John XXIII, Paul VI, and John Paul II; the Second Vatican Council; the beginning of lay movements; the emergence of charismatic persons like Dorothy Day and Mother Theresa; ecumenical episodes; and that is to say nothing of the world wars and Catholic involvement in them. These have been moments of enormous importance. Yet the reform of the liturgy has had such an extraordinarily long-lasting influence on us because through new, regular practices the reform has given us new ways of being.

Day after day, Sunday after Sunday, a continuous revolutionary process has occurred in which we have shifted through a set of practices our self-understanding as a people before God. The surety of unchangeable rubrics, the "universality" of the Latin language, the ethos of mystery, the reverence for the sacred species, and the priest as worthy intercessor at the altar of sacrifice were all important values that we safeguarded as we worshiped each week. These were engaged by other claims of ongoing renewal: the vernacular and the appreciation of local custom, the ethos of welcome and communion, the priest's call to communal prayer, and the mutual support of a shared vocation of discipleship.

The strict boundaries that defined us as Catholics before the Second Vatican Council were operative in the liturgical actions we practiced. Among those boundaries was the altar rail that physically, spiritually, and emotionally kept us at a distance from the altar. Even more remote was the host itself, an object of such veneration that we could never let it touch our hands. Those boundaries reinforced our own self-understanding.

Now the dominant virtues of obedience, reverence, and awe are replaced by love, community, and service. And so, as we turn to the liturgy, we will see how and where the grace of our merciful God leads us.

In the name of the Father . . .

We mark ourselves at the beginning and end of each liturgy with the same gesture. We identify ourselves by a sign that constitutes us as saved. It is the most fundamental mark of Christian worship. It frames not only the liturgy but our lives: We begin our Christian lives in baptism, first being signed with the cross, and in the sacrament of the sick we are anointed in the same sign at the end of our lives.

The cross is, above all, a sign of gift. By the gift of Christ's redemptive death on the cross we are saved and constituted as God's people. The German moral theologian Klaus Demmer argues that the cross must make a real difference in our lives. Specifically, it frees us, as Paul wrote, from sin and death. This freedom is not a conceptual one. Rather, we need to see that guilt and shame should have no lasting claim on our lives. Guilt and shame have no lasting claim on us, not because we are good but because Christ has taken away our sins. When we sign ourselves by the cross, we are getting ourselves in the practice of seeing that we have been set free from guilt so as to be free to live for ourselves and for others. Similarly, by the cross we are free of the lasting claim of death. When we sign ourselves by the cross, do we see our fears as taken away?

We need to become more aware of the effect that the practice of signing ourselves can have. It is a sign not only of being claimed by Christ but also a sign of identifying ourselves with his freedom from sin and death so as to serve one another. It is the sign of our liberation.

One of the horrendous twists in history has been, then, when Christians have used the cross to shame, imprison, exile, torture, or otherwise harm other persons. As sign of the gift of our liberation, it is above all an expression of God's mercy. That we Christians have used the cross as an instrument to claim our righteousness and other's wickedness is the great Christian obscenity. Whenever we separate our understanding of the cross from God's mercy, we inevitably risk again morally deplorable conduct, for we forget how our righteousness was won.

The liturgy, then, leads us from the sign of the cross to God's mercy.

Let us call to mind our need for God's mercy . . .

In doing so, we recognize what is being offered to us time and again: God's mercy. But here we call to mind our need for it. Reminding ourselves of our need for God's mercy keeps us from believing that we are much better than we are.

True Christians realize that falling on God's mercy is a good practice. It reminds us both how much we need God and how rich God's offering of mercy is. By invoking mercy we enter into the history of God, for God's relationship with us is always through mercy: By mercy we were saved, through mercy we are sanctified.

In the world of God's mercy we have enough of the loving light of God to consider what we have been and have done, individually and collectively.

I am always struck by the saints—the more they knew God and the more they knew themselves, the more they realized a need for God's mercy. Dorothy Day, for instance, became more and more surprised as she aged and grew in grace at how morally awful she was. This was not an awfulness based on any lack of self-esteem, but rather based on the sure love of God that let her see her true self. Indeed, as we begin the millennium, we need only the grace to see who we really are to realize our need for God's mercy.

Let us with all God's Church give God glory . . .

By entering into the world of God's mercy, our first response as sinners who have been saved is to give God glory. Rather than being fixed on ourselves, we surrender together to our God who delivers us. Giving God praise, we stand together realizing that as we look forward to the future we can only do it together if our focus is on the One whose nature is mercy.

· 17 ·

The Liturgy of the Word

$\mathscr{B}$efore the liturgy begins, each member of the community enters the church with different dispositions. No two have the same expectations, and each one savors the liturgy differently from the other. While no church-goer ever participates in the liturgy because of only one attractive feature, almost everyone draws consolation from particular aspects of the liturgy.

For some, the overall ritual of the liturgy itself is what brings them into proximity with God. They experience a sense of the holy, of devotion, and of the possibility of transformation through the beauty of the ritual as it moves from the first sign of the cross until the final blessing. For others the Eucharistic prayer, the prayer of the faithful, and the prayer after Communion offer avenues for communal prayer that can only be found in the parish liturgy. For still others, the Scripture readings and the homily provide insight and illumination, enough to nourish the Christian soul for days. Others have a devotion to Communion, looking with expectation to the moment when they actually receive the body and blood of Christ. Yet others have a sense of incorporation as they actively participate in a worshiping community, as they sing in the choir, greet other parishioners, proclaim the Word, or serve as extraordinary ministers of the Eucharist.

The Eucharistic liturgy is, then, a training ground that helps people enter into union with God. Through a variety of practices the church leads the community into different possible experiences with the Creator, Redeemer, and Sanctifier. Recognizing that we each encounter God in multitudinous ways, the church provides a liturgy with several modes for meeting the living God. It offers the worshiping community a host of opportunities. Thus, the liturgy of the Word forms us as a people responding to the initiative of God.

MANIPULATING GOD

Many years ago in Rome, I was participating in a group reflection on prayer. We were religious from all over the city and we knew one another well. There were several older religious in the group; most of them were models of joy, love, fidelity, and service, and they were very well loved. There was one, however, who was miserable and who perpetually manipulated her own community by her very dominating dispositions. (Many people living in religious communities or in rectories know well how one particular, miserable person can effectively hold the others hostage.)

We were asked by the group leader to tell the dominant image of God that we had when we prayed. Not surprisingly, different answers were given. As a doctoral student, I prayed to the forgiving God of the Prodigal Son. Another group member talked about the Spirit who freed her soul. Another, a grade-school teacher, talked about Jesus, the preacher of parables. An exciting collection of images of God were offered, and we began to see God's many faces. It was quite impressive to see the variety of ways God leads us.

The miserable one, however, had not yet spoken. Finally the leader pressed her. "I have always prayed to the infant Jesus." We sat stunned. "Always?" "Always!" This eighty-year-old nun had encountered God as a baby. "What does he say to you?" "He's a baby, he can't talk!" she snapped. "Well, what do you do?" "I take care of him. I change his diapers, burp him, let others visit with him. When their time is up, I send them away." No one said anything.

I saw how this person never let God speak to her. She had infantilized God, kept God in a crib, pampered God. She had such a powerless image of God that she never let God be God. Her prayer "freed" her, in turn, to dominate her own community, whom she controlled not only in their community rooms, but also in her own prayer when she became the infant's gatekeeper. Her prayer was her warrant of manipulation.

For years I remembered that afternoon when one person showed how well she could domesticate God. It was not until years later, however, that I saw the ways in which I was not much different than she. I too domesticated God, though surely my images were more sophisticated than hers. In fact, we all do. We make God into a series of nice convenient icons, put them up on a shelf, light a candle, and sigh relief that God has not escaped our clutches and become ... well ... God. We become, throughout our lives, experts in trapping God in imaginative exercises where God becomes a convenient object of our fantasy.

I think of this insight every time I prepare to preach. I rehearse to myself the first commandment and pray for the grace to heed it: "Let God be God." I try to let the readings speak. I try not to inhibit them with my own need to make them manageable, safe, in their place. Instead, I try to get the narrative right.

GETTING THE STORY OF JESUS RIGHT

The Protestant theologian Stanley Hauerwas claims that the true task of the Christian is to get the story of Jesus right. Hauerwas looks, for instance, at the great question of Jesus, "Who do the people say that I am?" Peter tells Jesus of a number of attributions. "But you, who do you say that I am?" Jesus asks Peter directly. Peter gets the title right. But once Jesus explains what the narrative of the Christ is, Peter admonishes him. Peter does not want the true story; he prefers his own icon, his nice homespun Messiah who is fun for fishing, miracles, and dinners. There is no suffering in the agenda Peter himself has set. Because of that, Peter does not get the story of Jesus right. In fact, throughout the Gospel, Peter has difficulty getting the narrative right (when he tries to send the people home hungry, keep the children from Jesus, use the sword to defend Jesus in the Garden, etc.). The more Peter tries to keep inconvenience, vulnerability, and suffering out of the story, the farther Peter moves away from the true narrative.

Of neither the nun in my opening story nor of Peter can we say, "There but for the grace of God go I." No, we are all Peters. Like him, we need to become a disciple, we need to learn from the Gospel the true story. After all, Peter, the prototypical disciple, teaches us just how difficult it is to get the story right. Rather than avoiding Peter, we need to see Peter in ourselves so that eventually, like Peter after the Pentecost, praying on the roof, we become suspicious of ourselves and allow ourselves to become open to the mystery of God. We need to recognize that, like Peter, we want a convenient narrative. And, like him, we can only be truly freed and healed and redeemed when the narrative is right.

That's why preaching the Word is so essential to the liturgy.

FOUR STEPS TO TAKE

How then do we get the story right? I suggest four steps. First, we need to remember the words of the great German Lutheran preacher and theologian Dietrich Bonhoeffer, who spoke about the danger of cheap grace. We need to recognize the triple costliness of our redemption, of grace, and of discipleship. Watering down the Gospel, making the Word convenient, or domesticating God cheapens the *new life* we have been given. We must always convey how dear the story of Jesus is.

Second, we must also recognize how burdened the people of God already are. As ministers of the Word, we are not called to browbeat the congregation, but to console it. Any available pastor knows the tangible complex concerns that affect members of the community. In that light, pastors try to attend to their community's needs. But they do so by conveying the narrative of Jesus as it really appears.

These two insights work in tandem. They keep us from compromising the Gospel and from being inattentive to the community.

The third insight reminds those of us who preach of our need to preach to ourselves. We must recognize that, like Peter, we have still not gotten the narrative right: We have to recognize the personal biases that prompt us to place obstacles in the way of the full message of Jesus. We need also to see how effective the Gospel can be in liberating us, for the more we recognize the true narrative of Jesus, the more we witness to our redemption. When we can testify to the effectiveness of the Gospel, we become true preachers of the Word.

Finally, we need to recognize that effectiveness is an ongoing process. Too many times we hear preachers tell the story of their conversion, as if it were complete! How much better we witness when we honestly testify to the modest ways in which we follow a God who patiently beckons us forward and to the more modest fact that much of the journey still stretches before us.

The Word of God is constantly forming us, wanting us to listen to it, so that we can be transformed by it. As the liturgy moves forward, we are called as a community to confess our faith, a faith shared by others who have heard the Word and kept it.

· 18 ·

The Liturgy of the Eucharist

Let us stand and confess our faith . . .

The congregation's first response to the Scripture heard and preached is the church's confession of its creed. It is the community's great "Amen!" to the liturgy of the Word. The creed focuses on God by centering exclusively on the three persons of the Trinity and on what the Trinity has done for us. By proclaiming our faith, we reflect on the God who made, saves, and delivers us. We recall God's deeds, in particular, God's mercy.

I define mercy as the willing disposition to enter into the chaos of another. Through reciting the creed, we see how God acts mercifully. God the Father subdues the chaos of the universe and makes heaven and earth. The Only Son enters into our world and becomes flesh. For our sake, Jesus suffers, dies, and is buried. On the third day, God raises him up. Christ becomes our judge; the Holy Spirit is the giver of life. Together in the Trinity, God is our merciful provider.

By confessing God's greatness at liturgy, we also reflect on how God is three persons in one: Father, Son, and Holy Spirit. For all of our contemporary talk of relationality, nothing compares to the church's ancient, trinitarian understanding of God. When we realize that God is three-in-one, we recognize that we, too, made in the image of God, are essentially relational. What is more, we are called to be like God, that is, merciful. For this reason, two tasks immediately follow the profession of faith in the liturgy: the prayer of the faithful and the collection. By these specific actions, all who worship demonstrate how humanity reflects the image of God, namely, that all people are intimately related to one another and all are called to be merciful, to show mercy.

99

In the prayer of the faithful, members of the church place their needs before God. Here is the reason many people come to worship. Burdened with genuine concerns (a marriage in trouble, a sick child, financial worries, a dying relative), worshipers at this phase of the liturgy may consider their fears and dreads and convert them into expressions of hope. In the face of a dying relative, for instance, the church calls on God for deliverance from sickness and death. Here is the moment when those facing sadness, turmoil, threat, anxiety, and pain, turn to God with confidence to utter their prayer of need and expectation. In the prayer of the faithful, individual members of the church enter into the community of hope.

The community also considers the needs of the entire church and world, moving beyond individual and local needs to embrace universal concerns. We call to mind those persons suffering from war, poverty, disaster, tyranny, and in so doing, stand, like God, in solidarity with the world. In the prayer of the faithful, we enter into the struggles of the world's poor, blighted, forgotten, making their needs ours.

Vigilance regarding the needs of others that is articulated in prayer leads naturally to the collection. Today, churches see the collection as a serious action that integrates the Christian response to the Scripture being preached and the prayers being raised. The collection is an absolute necessity in the liturgy because our concerns for the welfare of others cannot be solely subsumed under prayerfulness. For just as the spiritual works of mercy are coupled with the corporal works, so are our prayers coupled with the collection. Together, the prayers of the faithful and the collection make up our response to God's mercy as proclaimed to us in the Gospel and narrated in the creed. When we practice these corporal and spiritual works of mercy, we more fully become the image of the God whom we confess.

This desire to become more fully the image of God by recognizing our relatedness and by practicing mercy takes place to the extent that we remember, in the creed and the liturgy of the Word, what God has done for us. Remembrance, recognition, and mercy are intimately at work in this portion of the liturgy. These three practices prepare us to celebrate the next phase of the liturgy, in which the Eucharistic prayer is itself a memorial, a remembrance made present, a recognition made evident, and a mercy made real.

The Lord be with you . . .

Since memory is our most affective rational activity, remembrance is always heartfelt. Years ago, a friend in Italy reminded me that the Italian word for "remember" is *ricordare*, to bring back to the heart. The preface, like the Eucharistic prayer, is a narrative designed to awaken our hearts to what God has accomplished in Christ. For this reason, I often think of the Eucharistic prayer as functioning much like the discourse between Jesus and the disciples of Emmaus. In that discourse, the disciples first learned from Christ how all that had been foretold necessarily came to pass in the suffering, death, and resurrection of Jesus. Then, in the breaking of the bread they recognize the One who has set their hearts on fire.

The Eucharistic prayer helps us hear the narrative and recognize that we are characters in it. As with the disciples of Emmaus, we hear the story not only of what Christ has done, but what he has done for us. As we pray the Eucharistic prayer, we become participants in the drama of salvation history. Like the Emmaus disciples, we need to be instructed in salvation history so that at the breaking of the bread our eyes will be opened and we will be able to recognize who stands behind the story that has been told.

The Eucharistic prayer is central for training our hearts to learn the depth of God's commitment to us. It contains an instructive story that helps us remember again and again what God has done for us. But it is a lesson in the form of a prayer. For even in the telling of the deeds of God, God graces us with understanding so that we can grasp the story. Not only does the recounting of it make us participants in it, but through our prayer the story becomes real again. Praying the narrative moves salvation history forward into the very community gathered at Eucharist. The Eucharistic prayer is "effective" in the way sacraments are: Through it God makes salvation history present. Gathered in Christ's name, we experience Christ in our midst. The Eucharistic prayer accomplishes exactly what it narrates, making us the people of God, called, redeemed, and saved.

For this reason the community's responses are especially important. Members of the community are called to lift up their hearts and give thanks. They exclaim, "Holy, Holy, Holy," proclaiming the entrance of Jesus Christ himself. At the consecration, they proclaim the mystery of faith, using the same kerygma as the disciples did centuries ago. As the prayer comes to a close, they witness to the doxology in which Christ unites all things into himself. At that moment of union, they utter the great "Amen!" ratifying in the present what Christ has accomplished now and forever. Only in light of this Eucharistic prayer, then, are we ready to break the bread and drink from the cup, to enter into communion and have our eyes opened.

· 19 ·

Communion

Lamb of God, you take away the sins of the world, have mercy on us . . .

𝒯hroughout the history of devotional literature, the virtue of hope has always held central place. Good Christians read devotional books and practice piety in order to be supported in their hope in God. And, like any good virtue, hope stands between two extremes, despair and presumption. Our age is riddled with both of these vices.

Despair is rampant in two main ways: in the meaninglessness so many find in contemporary life and in the pervasive agnosticism that cuts across the industrialized world. In the post-Christian era, our secular cultures have anesthetized us to any fear or concern about despair, making meaninglessness a bearable absurdity and unbelief a de rigueur feature of life in the modern age.

But if contemporary secular culture is responsible for giving despair a comfortable home, our contemporary popular theological culture has made presumption an acceptable vice. Nowhere is this more apparent than in the inane assumption that we are all unquestionably to be rewarded with eternal life. While theologically there are ample grounds on which to insist on universal salvation, still for sixteen centuries it has been held that despite the *offer* of universal salvation, most people reject it by the lives they lead. Now, I am not suggesting that most of us are damned, as Augustine, Aquinas, and most major theologians in the distant past believed. Rather, just as I am stunned by Augustine's assumption of *massa damnata,* similarly I am struck by the contemporary *massa sanctificata.*

After casting off three centuries of neoscholastic moral theology, which inhibited the Christian conscience with its singular focus on the avoidance of sin, our age has developed a positive, developmentally oriented

moral theology but has never proposed an adequate notion of sin. Moreover, in the shadow of those three centuries, we have insisted on the goodness of humanity without acknowledging, concurrently, humanity's personal and collective wickedness. Although the preceding three centuries
proposed an eschatological vision in which harsh judgment always trumped
loving mercy, our eschatological vision, which ignores sin and insists on our
goodness, leaves us without need even for mercy. Today, the Last Judgment
is seen as our vindication, not because God's loving mercy delivers us
(which is what modern theologians do teach), but because we have been so
good in living our lives.

I admit to some exaggeration here, but there is considerable truth
in the main point. While cutting my theological teeth on Dietrich Bonhoeffer, I became convinced of two things: my own wickedness and the
cost of Christ's redemption. Both must be put against so much in our
pop theological culture today that cultivates cheap grace and that leaves
presumption an unquestionably valid attitude.

The liturgy can awaken us from this complacency, urging us to acknowledge our need for mercy so that we may enter into communion
with the One who saves us, wretches that we are.

This is the Lamb of God . . .

In the Catholic tradition, we understand that our pilgrimage comes to an
end in union with God. Union with God is what we understand to be the
ultimate purpose to our existence. Whether we think of the catechism, our
devotional heritage, scholastic writing, or most appropriately, the Gospels,
we have been rightly taught that God has made us to be in union with God.

Thomas Aquinas reminds us that on earth we experience, through
charity, that union with God. Aquinas insisted that the charity we have
on earth is the same as what we will have in heaven. This extraordinary
assertion means that we *already* have union with God. For Thomas, union
on earth is most perfectly experienced in the Eucharist.

Union takes place in the communion of the Eucharist. Like the disciples at Emmaus whose eyes were open, we come into union with Christ
and with one another as we participate in the Eucharistic meal. In fact, as I
argued in the last chapter, the Eucharistic prayer should prepare us for the
Emmaus experience of having our eyes opened. When our eyes are opened,
we experience the deep love, or unitive dimension, of the Eucharist.

It is important to focus on four particular insights leading up to that experience.

1. God never intrudes, but invites; we are free to accept or reject the invitation.

Union with God is only made possible by God. We cannot enter into union except through God's own invitation. God never enters into our lives, however, unless we accept the invitation. God so respects human freedom that God actually allows us either to ignore or to accept God's invitation. In every season of our lives—in loneliness, grief, illness, confusion, and joy—God offers to be with us, offers the gift of real presence. Yet the degree to which God enters our lives is singularly up to us to permit. When we receive Christ's body and blood at Communion, we accept the invitation of God to enter into union.

Whenever I preside at liturgy, I remind myself of the variety of ways that we Catholics gather for worship. We enter the door with an extraordinary range of concerns on our collective mind, and we each come into the Eucharist with our own agenda. Some come worried about work, health, or a loved one. Some come looking for spiritual satisfaction. Some come out of devotion. Some come specifically to pray in thanksgiving. Some come from lonely apartments, others from maddeningly busy households. We all come together, however, for the nourishment of the Word, prayer, Eucharist, and community. We come as a people hoping that our hungers will be sated by the presence of God. In a word, we come to enter into union with God.

2. The presence of God is illuminating.

Regardless of what is going on in our lives, the first sign of the presence of God is light. The Christian tradition has always taught that the first sign of God's presence is an ability to see in a way that we never before could. Almost every devotional text insists that before union with God, the Christian experiences illumination.

Illumination is basically what the Scriptures, the homily, and the Eucharistic prayer accomplish. Our eyes, ears, hearts, and souls are opened so that we may willingly seek to be in union with God. In the presence of God we see our own condition; we see more clearly our sinfulness and our need for mercy; we see the blessedness of our lives and reasons for gratitude; and we see our grief and longing to be reunited with those who have gone before us. In that illumination we stand and hear, "Behold the Lamb of God."

3. Our union with God never replaces our relationships with one another.

As we move toward the unitive, we realize that union with God never nullifies in any way our experiences with one another. God respects us, only entering our lives as they really are. God keeps intact the bonds of friendship and the longings for companionship. Thus, persons who are lonely and wish for more human company do not find in Communion that their loneliness is resolved. Companioned by Christ, they recognize that they are not abandoned yet they still yearn for friends. Likewise those who grieve know that God's presence does not end their grief, but rather preserves it. Dietrich Bonhoeffer makes this point poignantly when he writes,

> Nothing can make up for the absence
> of someone we love.
>
> And it would be wrong to try to find a substitute.
> We must simply hold out and see it through.
> That sounds very hard at first,
> but at the same time
> it is a great consolation.
> For the gap—as long as it remains unfulfilled—
> preserves the bond between us.
>
> It is nonsense to say that
> God fills the gap.
> God does not fill it.
> But on the contrary, keeps it empty
> and so helps us to keep alive
> our former communion with each other
> even at the cost of pain.

In the unity of Communion, we do not enter into God's world; God enters into ours. The Incarnation plays itself out yet again and never destroys the human in the process. In union with God, the variety of human relationships remains intact, and, like us, the relationships are respected and become consecrated by the abiding presence of God.

4. Union with God.

In union with God, then, we experience God's entry into our lives and that entry, premiered by illumination, is above all consoling. When we receive Communion, God's self enters into us and inasmuch as God is mercy, rescuing us from chaos, God consoles us. The concerns we bring to the liturgy are not magically taken away. Instead, God enters into them, abiding with us as God pledges to be with us until the end.

We can appreciate the remarkable insight by Augustine that God is closer to us than we are to ourselves. In union with God, the consoling presence of God is no longer felt as another. Rather, it is felt intimately as at one with us.

The Lord be with you . . .

During my years as a doctoral student in Rome, I occasionally went to Mass at the Church of San Andrea del Valle. There, to a congregation of about twenty, after Communion and before the final blessing, the celebrant would say in a familiar way, "You are going to your homes and I to mine, but before I go, I have one more thing to say to you." He would pause and we, in great expectation, would await his words knowing exactly what he would say, because he concluded the liturgy with these words every evening. We paused, savoring the words that he eventually uttered, the very words we longed to hear, "The Lord be with you."

Index

109

About the Author

𝒯r. James F. Keenan, S.J., entered the New York Province of the Society of Jesus in 1970 and was ordained a priest in 1982. He was graduated with a bachelor's degree in English and Philosophy from Fordham University (1976) and a master's of divinity from Weston Jesuit School of Theology (1982). He studied moral theology at the Gregorian University in Rome with Frs. Josef Fuchs and Klaus Demmer and received a licentiate (1984) and a doctorate (1988).

He taught at Fordham University from 1987–1991 and has been teaching at Weston Jesuit School of Theology since 1991. He was consultant to the National Catholic Conference of Bishops for the revision of the *Ethical and Religious Directives for Catholic Health Care Institutions* (1988–1995) and a group leader of the U.S. Surgeon General's Task Force on Responsible Sexual Conduct (2000–2002). He has been on the editorial board of *Theological Studies* since 1991 and the board of directors of the Society of Christian Ethics (2001–2005). He is editor of the Moral Traditions series at Georgetown University Press.

The Works of Mercy: The Heart of Catholicism is Father Keenan's newest book. His earlier works include *Goodness and Rightness in Thomas Aquinas's Summa Theologiae, Virtues for Ordinary Christians, Commandments of Compassion, Jesus and Virtue Ethics* (with Dan Harrington), and, more recently, *Moral Wisdom: Lessons and Texts from the Catholic Tradition*. He is now writing a book with Dr. Jon Fuller, S.J., on HIV/AIDS and the Catholic Church.

He edited *Practice What You Preach: Virtues, Ethics and Power in the Lives of Pastoral Ministers and Their Congregations* which won the Catholic

Press Award for best work in Pastoral Theology (2000) and *Catholic Ethicists on HIV/AIDS Prevention* which won the best work in ethics from the Jesuit Honor Society, Alpha Sigma Nu, (2003). He has published more than 200 essays, articles, and reviews in more than twenty-five international journals. He has been a fellow both at the Institute of Advanced Studies at The University of Edinburgh (1994) and the Center of Theological Inquiry, Princeton (1995, 1996).

He has been adjunct professor at both the Gregorian University in Rome (2000, 2002) and Loyola School of Theology in Manila (2001, 2003). He held the Tuohy Chair at John Carroll University, Cleveland (1999) and presently holds the Gasson Chair at Boston College (2003–2005).

Organizing and Managing Information Resources on Your Campus

Polley Ann McClure, Editor

Organizing and Managing Information Resources on Your Campus

EDUCAUSE

Leadership Strategies No. 7

JOSSEY-BASS
A Wiley Imprint
www.josseybass.com

Published by Jossey-Bass
A Wiley Imprint
989 Market Street, San Francisco, CA 94103-1741   www.josseybass.com

This book is part of the Jossey-Bass Higher and Adult Education Series.

Jossey-Bass books and products are available through most bookstores. To contact
Jossey-Bass directly, call our Customer Care Department within the U.S. at
(800) 956-7739, outside the U.S. at (317) 572-3993 or fax (317) 572-4002.

Jossey-Bass also publishes its books in a variety of electronic formats. Some content
that appears in print may not be available in electronic books.

Library of Congress Cataloging-in-Publication Data

Organizing and managing information resources on your campus /
Polley Ann McClure, editor.—1st ed.
    p. cm.—(EDUCAUSE leadership strategies; no. 7)
(The Jossey-Bass higher and adult education series)
Includes bibliographical references and index.
  ISBN 0-7879-6665-7 (pbk.)
  1. Education, Higher—Effect of technological innovations on—United
States. 2. Information technology—United States—Management.
I. McClure, Polley A. II. EDUCAUSE (Association) III. Series. IV. Series:
The Jossey-Bass higher and adult education series
  LB2395.7.O75 2003
  378'.00285—dc21   2003008170

Printed in the United States of America
PB Printing 10 9 8 7 6 5 4 3 2 1   FIRST EDITION

The EDUCAUSE Leadership Strategies series addresses critical themes related to information technology that will shape higher education in the years to come. The series is intended to make a significant contribution to the knowledge academic leaders can draw upon to chart a course for their institutions into a technology-based future. Books in the series offer practical advice and guidelines to help campus leaders develop action plans to further that end. The series is developed by EDUCAUSE and published by Jossey-Bass. The sponsorship of PricewaterhouseCoopers LLP makes it possible for EDUCAUSE to distribute complimentary copies of books in the series to more than 1,800 EDUCAUSE member institutions, organizations, and corporations.

EDUCAUSE

EDUCAUSE is a nonprofit association with offices in Boulder, Colorado, and Washington, D.C. The association's mission is to advance higher education by promoting the intelligent use of information technology. EDUCAUSE activities include an educational program of conferences, workshops, seminars, and institutes; a variety of print and on-line publications; strategic/policy initiatives such as the National Learning Infrastructure Initiative, the Net@EDU program, and the EDUCAUSE Center for Applied Research; and extensive Web-based information services.

EDUCAUSE

- provides professional development opportunities for those involved with planning for, managing, and using information technologies in colleges and universities
- seeks to influence policy by working with leaders in the education, corporate, and government sectors who have a stake in the transformation of higher education through information technologies
- enables the transfer of leading-edge approaches to information technology management and use that are developed and shared through EDUCAUSE policy and strategy initiatives
- provides a forum for dialogue between information resources professionals and campus leaders at all levels
- keeps members informed about information technology innovations, strategies, and practices that may affect their campuses, identifying and researching the most pressing issues

Current EDUCAUSE membership includes more than 1,800 campuses, organizations, and corporations. For up-to-date information about EDUCAUSE programs, initiatives, and services, visit the association's Web site at www.educause.edu, send e-mail to info@educause.edu, or call 303-449-4430.

PRICEWATERHOUSE COOPERS

PricewaterhouseCoopers is a leading provider of professional services to institutions of higher education, serving a full range of educational institutions—from small colleges to large public and private universities to educational companies.

PricewaterhouseCoopers (www.pwcglobal.com) is the world's largest professional services organization, drawing on the knowledge and skills of more than 150,000 people in 150 countries to help clients solve complex business problems and measurably enhance their ability to build value, manage risk, and improve performance in an Internet-enabled world.

PricewaterhouseCoopers refers to the member firms of the worldwide PricewaterhouseCoopers organization.

Contents

Acknowledgments

First and foremost, I thank the chapter authors who contributed their enthusiasm, time, and expertise to the creation of this book. I also acknowledge the outstanding teamwork among the authors and the EDUCAUSE staff: Julia Rudy and Cynthia Golden, especially, and Mark Luker for lending his technical knowledge to the development of some of the chapters. Everyone pulled together and made my job as editor fun. Editors of books expect expert knowledge from their contributing authors and expert skills from editorial staff, but the collaborative spirit and can-do attitudes that pervaded this work made my work as editor a pleasure.

April 2003   POLLEY ANN MCCLURE

The Authors

Polley Ann McClure is vice president for information technologies and professor in the Ecology and Evolutionary Biology Department at Cornell University. Prior to her appointment at Cornell, she held similar positions at the University of Virginia and Indiana University. McClure has spoken and published widely in the biological literature and, more recently, about information technology management in higher education. She served as a member and officer of the boards of Educom and CAUSE and was the first chair of the EDUCAUSE board of directors, facilitating the merger of Educom and CAUSE. McClure has a B.A. in zoology and a Ph.D. in ecology from the University of Texas at Austin and an M.A. in ecology from the University of Montana.

Carole A. Barone is vice president of EDUCAUSE, where her responsibilities include a focus on the National Learning Infrastructure Initiative. Before joining EDUCAUSE in 1998, she was associate vice chancellor for information technology at the University of California at Davis, and prior to that she was vice president for information systems and computing at Syracuse University. Barone speaks and writes extensively on the relationship between technology and change. She coedited *Technology-Enhanced Teaching and Learning: Leading and Supporting the Transformation on Your*

Campus (Jossey-Bass, 2001) as Volume 5 in the EDUCAUSE Leadership Strategies series. Barone holds an M.A. and Ph.D. from the Maxwell School of Citizenship and Public Affairs at Syracuse University.

Brian L. Hawkins is president of EDUCAUSE. Previously, he was chief information officer and later senior vice president for academic planning and administrative affairs at Brown University. Prior to that, he was associate vice president for academic affairs at Drexel University, where he was responsible for general academic planning and also oversaw the academic program that was the first in the nation to integrate technology use throughout the curriculum. Hawkins is a management professor by training and is the author of three books and many articles in the areas of organizational behavior and technology and academic planning. He received his bachelor's and master's degrees from Michigan State University and his Ph.D. from Purdue University.

Ronald A. Johnson is vice president, chief information officer/chief technology officer, and faculty member at the University of Washington, where his responsibilities include computing and networking infrastructure for the campus and medical centers. He has played a significant role in each generation of national networking in the United States. Among other current activities, Johnson is a principal for the National LightRail effort and the Pacific Northwest Gigapop, as well as its Pacific Wave international peering point. He also serves as a director on a number of boards, including CENIC, the IEEAF, KEXP-FM, and the ResearchChannel. Johnson holds degrees from the University of Chicago and the University of Southern California.

Alan McCord is senior director for planning and coordination for the Information Technology Central Services unit of the University of Michigan and an adjunct faculty member at the University of Michigan School of Information. He has also served the university as associate university chief information officer and director of operations management. Prior to his position at Michigan, he served as executive director of University Computing at Eastern Michigan University and held administrative positions at Wayne State University and Oakland Community College. McCord is active in EDUCAUSE and serves on its Evolving Technologies Committee. He holds a B.S. from the University of Michigan and an M.Ed. and Ph.D. from Wayne State University.

Jack McCredie is associate vice chancellor and chief information officer at the University of California, Berkeley. Before going to Berkeley in 1992, he worked in the research group at Digital Equipment Corporation, served as president of Educom, and was vice provost for computing and planning at Carnegie Mellon University. McCredie was a charter member of the board of directors of the Corporation for Education Network Initiatives in California (CENIC), where he served as the vice chair of the board, and he is currently chair of the Program Steering Committee for the Digital California Project. He has a B.S. and M.S. in engineering from Yale University and a Ph.D. from Carnegie Mellon University.

Marilyn Ayres McMillan is associate provost and chief information technology officer at New York University. In that capacity, she leads the delivery and evolution of university-wide services, infrastructure, policies, and plans for information technology and related activities and is a member of the university's leadership team. Before joining NYU, she held numerous information technology leadership roles during nearly twenty years at the Massachusetts Institute of Technology and subsequently at Stanford University, with earlier information technology experience in government and private industry. McMillan served on the board of directors of CAUSE and various CAUSE committees and was one of the founding faculty members of the EDUCAUSE Institute Leadership Program. She is a graduate of Douglass College at Rutgers University in political science, with graduate work at Virginia Tech and Boston University.

Tracy Mitrano is policy adviser and director of the University Computer Policy and Law Program for the Office of Information Technologies at Cornell University. She has taught American political, social, and religious history at the University of Buffalo, women's and constitutional history at Syracuse University, and family and social policy at Cornell University. A member of the New York State Bar Association, she was in private practice for five years. Mitrano has a B.A. in English and history from the University of Rochester, a Ph.D. in American history from Binghamton University, and a law degree from Cornell Law School.

James G. Neal is vice president for information services and university librarian at Columbia University. Previously, he served as dean of university libraries at Johns Hopkins and Indiana universities. Neal has served on the Council and Executive Board of the American Library Association and on the board and as president of the Association of Research Libraries, as well as on numerous international and national professional committees and task forces. His research and speaking interests include scholarly communication, intellectual property, digital library development, and organizational change. He received a B.A. in Russian studies from Rutgers University and an M.A. in history, M.S. in library science, and the Certificate in Advanced Librarianship from Columbia.

James I. Penrod is vice president for information systems and chief information officer at the University of Memphis. He previously served in similar positions at Pepperdine University, the University of Maryland at Baltimore, and California State University, Los Angeles. He also is a tenured graduate professor of Higher and Adult Education Leadership in the College of Education at Memphis. Penrod speaks frequently to regional and national audiences and has many publications related to information technology issues in higher education. He is a former board member of CAUSE and Educom and currently serves on the EDUCAUSE Nomination and Election Committee. He has a B.A. in mathematics from Harding University, an M.S. in biostatistics from Tulane, and an Ed.D. in institutional management from Pepperdine University.

Toby D. Sitko is a research fellow at the EDUCAUSE Center for Applied Research. She previously served as director of policy and planning for Information Technology Services at New York University, deputy executive director for information resources at the City University of New York Graduate Center, director of information technology customer services at the University of Houston, and assistant director for user support at Indiana University Bloomington. Sitko is on the faculty of the EDUCAUSE Leadership Institute, was a member of the EDUCAUSE Current Issues Committee, and was chair of the EDUCAUSE Publications Advisory Committee. With colleagues, Sitko publishes and delivers professional papers on various aspects of information technology leadership and management. She holds a B.A. in English and American literature from Queens College of the City University of New York and an M.A. in journalism from Indiana University.

David L. Smallen is vice president for information technology at Hamilton College, responsible for all planning, budgeting, and management of IT resources. While serving on both the CAUSE and Educom boards, he was a member of the committee that created the original *CAUSE/Educom Evaluation Guidelines for Institutional Information Technology Resources*. He currently codirects the COSTS project, an international effort for understanding the true costs of information technology support services. Smallen is a frequent speaker and contributor to the national literature on information technology and the winner of the 2000 EDUCAUSE Award for Leadership in the Profession. He holds a B.S. and an M.S. from the

State University of New York at Albany and a Ph.D. in mathematics from the University of Rochester.

R. David Vernon is director of information technology architecture in the Office of Information Technology at Cornell University. Prior to his position at Cornell, he held several appointments at Indiana University Computing Services. Vernon's wide range of experience and expertise includes data networking, research computing, student computing infrastructure, digital presentation technologies, messaging, mass-data-storage infrastructure, corporate relations, review of strategic initiatives, and security policy and implementation. At Cornell, he has published a series of papers that have led to broad discussion and acceptance of strategic IT issues on campus. Vernon has been a member of the NYSERnet Board of Directors since 2000. He received his B.A. from Earlham College.

Organizing and
Managing
Information
Resources on
Your Campus

Managing the Complexity of Campus Information Resources

Polley Ann McClure

In 1989, Brian Hawkins, who edited and introduced the book *Organizing and Managing Information Resources on Campus* (part of the Educom Strategies Series on Information Technology), and Ken King, who wrote the book's concluding remarks, both clearly saw higher education as being in the midst of a revolution. Citing the Carnegie Foundation for the Advancement of Teaching, Hawkins summarized the observation this way: "Higher education no longer merely anticipates a revolution in computer use; the revolution is under way" (p. 1).

Now, nearly fifteen years later, the turbulence of the computer revolution is subsiding. The revolution is not over by a long shot, but information technology (IT) has found its way into every aspect of higher education institutions, and we are beginning to deal with it as a "grown-up" instead of as the unruly youngster Hawkins and his contemporaries described in 1989.

The purpose of this book is to take a new look at the role of IT in higher education from the perspective of trying to be good managers of this major institutional resource. We will find ourselves addressing some of the same old questions, some of which will have new answers and some the same old answers. In addition, some new questions have arisen, and some old ones have grown in importance.

In grappling with both old and new questions, IT managers must take into account the tradition and culture of higher education as a social institution. Higher education is the environment within which the IT function has evolved and currently operates. This environment has shaped structures and practices, and it determines ways of thinking about future options. At the same time, all the other elements of colleges and universities are adapting to and being changed by IT. Some environmental influences and adaptations are common throughout higher education; others are particular to individual institutions. In this book, we think about the management of IT in this dynamic frame of reference, examining ways in which higher education, both generally and specifically, has shaped the present and will shape the future for our IT practices.

The Influence of Higher Education's Decentralized Structure

One significant characteristic of higher education in general is its stable self-protecting structure, as Clark Kerr (1980, p. 9) points out: "Taking, as a starting point, 1530, when the Lutheran Church was founded, some 66 institutions that existed then still exist today in the Western World in recognizable form: the Catholic Church, the Lutheran Church, the parliaments of Iceland and the Isle of Man, and 62 universities. . . . They have experienced wars, revolutions, depressions, and industrial transformations, and have come out less changed than almost any other segment of their societies."

Higher education institutions exhibit this persistence because of their political and economic isolation and because it is part of their mission to transcend social change, which they exist to analyze, record, communicate, and interpret (Bowen, 2001). Persistence results also from the nature of the structure of higher education, which has been described as loosely coupled anarchy. While this kind of structure contributes to an institution's survival, it also contributes to its inability to evolve quickly—to the frustration of many change agents. It is difficult for a relatively new and dynamic element such as IT to invade and find a comfortable place within a structure so resistant to change.

Calling higher education institutions loosely coupled is another way of saying that their subunits are highly independent. While some outside observers exhort these institutions to behave more like businesses and exhibit the directedness of corporations, the management options within the IT function are defined by the reality that institutions of higher learning run themselves more as communities of autonomous members than as hierarchical bodies. Individual colleges, even individual professors, often operate as autonomous elements, optimizing their own performance with little regard for that of other units within the institution. From one campus to another, internal economies may vary along a continuum from more centrally planned to highly entrepreneurial, but all are characterized by a concentration of economic power at the periphery. Indeed, institutional goals and priorities arise more often from the individual faculty, departments, schools, and colleges than from the president's office.

Consequently, institutional decision-making processes rely on broad representation and consensus rather than managerial prerogative. This approach to management, which is key to higher education institutions' success as creative and critical engines of ideas, does present challenges when it comes to deploying an institutional enterprise IT infrastructure.

The degree of centralization at any given institution is a fairly intractable, highly significant attribute to take into account in designing effective IT management strategies. For example, if only a small number of people can authorize practices for IT, decision making is relatively straightforward. The larger the number of individuals involved (the more decentralized the environment), the more complex the decision-making process is.

Along the same lines, greater centralization usually corresponds to easier, less expensive deployment of information systems supporting administrative processes, because these processes are generally more coherent and more widely understood and because the network itself is generally more coherent (less fragmented) than in highly decentralized environments.

In general, between the decentralized nature of higher education and the distributed nature of today's desktop computing, higher education institutions are battling powerful centrifugal forces. These forces work against true enterprise standards and the efficiencies they could yield. One of higher education's most important challenges is to develop specific mechanisms to resist the excessively disruptive effects of these forces.

The Influence of Financial Architecture

Another important environmental variable for IT managers is an institution's financial architecture. Two main types of models have emerged: the responsibility-centered model and the centrally planned model.

If the institution operates under a relatively responsibility-centered economy, in which constituent units have both income and expenditure responsibility (often referred to as "each tub on its own bottom"), the central IT function will tend toward fee-based services, and in many cases the constituent units will have greater autonomy in deciding how to provision themselves with IT services. Fee-based services often leave the door open for free choice, which can lead to greater heterogeneity and complexity.

If the institution operates more as a centrally planned economy with most funds coming into the central administration, which then allocates funds among units, IT services are more likely to be perceived as free goods. In this situation, it is easier to deploy standards, which can lead to a generally more coherent architecture.

The economic model in effect—whether central funding or dispersed responsibility for recapturing costs—colors all dimensions of IT management.

The Influence of History

Events and practices in an institution's history also shape thinking about how to manage the IT function. History can even have long-term effects on the way higher education institutions evaluate their management options. For example, some institutions exhibit a cannibalistic reaction to particularly successful IT functions. It is not unusual to see the best IT organizations taken down a notch by other elements of the institution. When these reactions are taking place, the IT manager has a different set of options and issues to contemplate than when the function is in favor.

Growth of the IT Function

Besides bearing in mind particular environmental influences—including degree of decentralization, type of financial architecture, and accumulation of historical events—we also need to remember how new the IT function is among the well-established functions in higher education institutions. Many colleges and universities in the United States have existed for more than a hundred years, while IT has been around for less than one-third of that time.

More important, during that short time, IT has grown faster than anyone in the field or in society at large imagined. At Cornell University, for example, between 1982 and 2002, the number of personal computers grew from probably fewer than 250 to well over 25,000, each with greater computational power than all of the computers on campus combined in 1982. Total computational power across campus went from something like 0.002 to somewhere around 12,900 gigaflops.

In 1982, modern high-speed data networking did not exist. Cornell had limited point-to-point connectivity, consisting mostly of "dumb" terminals attached to mainframes. The fastest modem speeds were 1,200 bits per second. Intercampus communication happened mainly through Bitnet, a popular store-and-forward network that operated at about 4,800 bits per second. Today, the university's fiber-optic gigabit backbone connects every computer on campus with at least switched 10/100 megabit per second bandwidth, and the connections to the Internet operate at more than 300 megabits per second.

Moreover, two decades ago, nothing like the World Wide Web existed. Today we take it for granted as an easy, intuitive tool for finding information of all kinds.

We have no records of volume of e-mail traffic in 1982, but we do know that Cornell published volume 1 of *A User's Guide to the Cornell MAIL System* that year. It seems safe to speculate that the volume of messages was well under 1 million that year. During the first nine months of 2002 alone, Cornell e-mail servers processed more than 250 million messages.

In 1982, it was almost exclusively scientific researchers who used the network and academic computational resources. Today, almost every student and employee at Cornell and everywhere else depends on the network to access important information, entertainment, and other people. Students have grown up in a networked, multimedia world. Their expectations about technology on campus are very different from those of students in 1982.

Twenty years ago, IT for the most part was the domain of the IT specialist. Today, no one in the academy can avoid taking some responsibility for its impact. Managers all over the institution "own" it. In managing the function, we must accept the reality that it is no longer a singular entity that anyone can directly control.

Growth of this magnitude has necessarily strained many fronts. As IT has forced its way into all facets of our institutions, it has displaced other priorities and caused us to change the way everyone on campus works. It has spawned entirely new academic disciplines. It has opened new approaches and ideas in almost every established field. This kind of growth raises many management issues, not the least of which is cost.

Cost Management

Computers and networks have been, and still are, very expensive. Because few institutions have found totally new funding sources for this purpose, in many cases resources have been taken away from other priorities to buy and support IT. For example, Cornell's central IT budget (minus telephone services) went from about $8.6 million in 1982—1.8 percent of the total expenditure budget—to $33.4 million in 2002, or 2.0 percent of the total.

Even as the central IT budget has encroached on other spending, IT expenditures outside the central organization have grown even more significantly. We do not have precise figures for the total IT expenditures at Cornell for 1982 or 2002, but we do know that approximately two-thirds of the technical IT staff at the university in 2002 are not in the central organization. If other noncentral IT expenses have grown proportional to the staff, the total percentage of university expenses is close to 6 percent for 2002.

Clearly, expenditures of this order deserve careful management. And we have learned a lot about how to budget and plan for IT costs. Early on, many administrators treated IT purchases as one-time expenditures, funded through year-end surplus funds or provided as gifts. Today, we all realize that each new computer will need to be replaced in three years, and each new capability will require care and feeding in perpetuity. We have become and need to continue to be long-term strategic thinkers with regard to managing costs.

Convergence of Technologies

Concurrent with IT's rapid growth, the elements of technology have been undergoing significant convergence. At one point, institutions provided access to movies and other illustrative materials through audiovisual centers. Meanwhile, the business functions received IT support through administrative computer centers, reporting usually through the chief financial officer, while the academic computer center, reporting to the provost, provided tools for research computation. Telephone service was purchased from the local Bell company; if it was provided on campus, the telecommunications department was usually part of business services. Each of these functions reported through a different vice-presidential line, and their respective technologies were completely different.

During the past two decades, these technologies, and in many cases their underlying protocols, have converged. As was the case with technology growth, this convergence initially caused great stress on organizations. With time, we have seen how to reorganize IT to take advantage of the underlying commonalities. Most campuses today have one or at most two central IT support organizations instead of four or five. The ongoing convergence of technologies will continue to drive IT organizational and management practices.

Evolution of the IT Organization

The IT support organization is not only consolidating but also maturing. Twenty years ago, the top positions were typically occupied by those whose concept of managing was mainly about being the sharpest technologist. Even a decade ago, IT units on campus were often little more than a collection of independent practitioners. Today, many of these units use formal planning and reporting mechanisms. Their leaders have had careers in the IT industry and are seasoned managers. These organizations have also grown on the soft side, with training, help desks, and communications taking respected places alongside direct hardware and software support.

As we emerge from the revolutionary period, central IT organizations are absorbing the campus utility functions of administrative systems and communications. If we can survive the enterprise resource planning phase, there is some reason to anticipate a period of stability in these functions, and during that time we may be able to improve on the efficiency of IT performance. Conversely, day-to-day instructional technology will probably evolve to be supported largely by the schools and colleges within universities, as has already happened with all except the highest-powered research computing. Institutions that have strategic agendas that depend on instructional and research computing will continue to support those elements at the institutional level.

Basic Elements of the IT Function

The IT function has the following basic elements (see Figure 1.1):

- The services delivered to the institution (for example, e-mail, payroll services, and electronic conferencing)

- The technologies (that is, the hardware and software) that deliver services

Figure 1.1. Elements of the IT Function

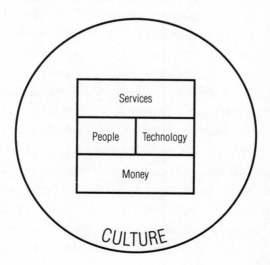

- The people who manage the services and technologies and support other people in their use

- The financial resources invested by the institution in the first three elements

- The institutional cultures that shape the other four elements

Only by considering all of these elements, and the ways in which they interact, can an institution effectively manage IT. The chapters that follow suggest ways to achieve alignment between these basic elements by implementing synergistic processes that enfold them all.

Tools for Managing the Basic Elements

The art of IT management is to design processes and structures that successfully combine the five basic elements. Ideally, the basic elements are managed through planning, organizing, funding, assessing, governing, and nurturing (see Figure 1.2).

Setting up these processes and structures is not something that is done regularly, and changing any one of them represents a major project in most organizational settings. We tend to think about them when the existing way of doing things quits working, when we have to change one element for some reason and that change raises questions about others, or when some truly new opportunity presents itself. In these situations, we need to make the major investment to redefine our strategies.

The chapters that follow provide many references, direct and indirect, to the five basic IT elements and the institutional processes for managing them. In Chapter Two, James Penrod describes the mechanisms of governance as they are designed to respond to other aspects of culture and environment. He calls special attention to the needed alignment between various governance and decision-making processes. James Neal and I examine options in Chapter

Figure 1.2. Institutional Process for Managing Elements of the IT Function

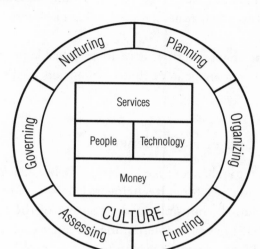

Three for structures to organize people under various cultural and environmental conditions.

In Chapter Four, David Smallen and Jack McCredie explore sustainable funding models for technology use and development in a variety of institutional settings. Next, in Chapter Five, Alan McCord helps us think about new mechanisms for acquiring IT services from internal or outside providers. These mechanisms will have major impacts on the other elements of institutional IT function.

Tracy Mitrano discusses in Chapter Six the governing aspect of policy, its formulation, and its relationship to institutional policy generally and some contemporary developments in IT policies specifically. In Chapter Seven, Ronald Johnson, Tracy Mitrano, and R. David Vernon look for ways to provide secure IT systems by managing people's behavior. Some of the mechanisms for doing this are technological; others are cultural.

Marilyn McMillan and Toby Sitko show that managing business continuity has become a university-wide priority, not simply a concern for technologists. They outline in Chapter Eight an approach for engaging all of the right people in the essentials of continuity planning and emergency preparedness. Finally, in Chapter Nine, Brian Hawkins and Carole Barone develop ideas about new forms of assessment.

All of the chapter authors contribute valuable perspectives on some aspect of management that IT managers deal with almost every day.

The IT Manager as Gardener

It is common to talk about reengineering higher education or elements of it, like teaching. Reengineering may be an idea that IT managers can use, but only in the context of the higher-level processes that I have been describing. An analogy I like to use is gardening. IT management is akin to planting seeds of ideas and waiting to see if any will germinate. If they do, we scurry around to find water and nutrients, and we try to keep the weeds at bay, so that the practices we need to encourage have a chance of taking hold. As they grow and develop, we are constantly called on to cultivate their soil and to stake and prune and protect them.

To take the analogy in a slightly different direction, the main challenge of the next decade will be harvesting the benefits from the profound institutional changes that have followed the computer revolution. Because this challenge is not about IT itself, IT leaders will play only a part in it—a less visible part than others, perhaps, but indispensable nonetheless. The big question we will need to address is this: How can we continue to deliver the infrastructure, applications, and services in the most efficient way possible to enable these institutional benefits? The answers offered in the following chapters are varied and inspiring.

References

Bowen, W. G. "At a Slight Angle to the Universe: The University in a Digitized, Commercialized Age." *ARL: A Bimonthly Report on Research Library*

Issues and Actions from ARL, CNI, and SPARC, no. 216. Washington,
    D.C.: Association of Research Libraries, Coalition of Networked Informa-
    tion, and Scholarly Publishing and Academic Resources Coalition, 2001.
Hawkins, B. "Managing a Revolution—Turning a Paradox into a Paradigm."
    In B. Hawkins (ed.), *Organizing and Managing Information Resources on
    Campus*. McKinney, Tex.: Academic Computing Publications, 1989.
Kerr, C. "Three Thousand Futures: The Next Twenty Years for Higher
    Education." In Carnegie Council on Policy Studies in Higher Educa-
    tion, *Three Thousand Futures: The Next Twenty Years for Higher Education*.
    San Francisco: Jossey-Bass, 1980.

Building an Effective Governance and Decision-Making Structure for Information Technology

James I. Penrod

One of the frequent difficulties that a campus chief information officer (CIO) encounters results from misunderstandings between governance and management. The following questions are pertinent when thinking about these difficulties in the context of higher education organizations: What is the role of a policy committee? How does that role relate to day-to-day decision making? Is information technology (IT) policy usually derived for the institution or the central technology group? What is the role of an advisory committee? Is the role of a CIO primarily in governance or management? How obligated is a CIO to heed the advice of a committee? This chapter provides a context for appropriate answers to such questions.

Issues for General Consideration

A number of variables, in combination and usually institutional specific, have a significant impact on what constitutes good governance and decision making: general institutional characteristics, sources and levels of funding, leadership style, formality of planning, organizational culture, decision-making style, and type of IT leadership structure.

Institutional Characteristics

Is the institution private or public? Private institutions usually have a more focused set of stakeholders and thus are able to articulate a unique mission more definitively. They typically have a simpler bureaucracy and can implement decisions more quickly. These elements affect what policy is derived, how decisions are made, and who makes them.

Is the organization research-intensive, comprehensive, or a liberal arts or community college? A research-intensive campus demands an IT infrastructure that is diverse and robust. At these institutions, across-the-board standards are less likely to be in place. Teaching is likely to be emphasized at comprehensive or liberal arts colleges or universities and community colleges; thus, proportionally, more faculty may be involved in IT areas related to teaching and learning than to infrastructure development.

What is the size of the college or university? Smaller institutions are likely more unified and less diverse, making it easier to reach a consensus decision. Midsize campuses may have more resources to bring to bear on an issue than smaller ones, but they may have a simpler bureaucracy than large institutions; therefore, the blend of factors may work in their favor. Large universities benefit from the scope of disciplines and accumulated human resources that enable a reservoir of knowledge that can be meaningful when tapped.

Characteristics such as these affect the organizational climate and culture, organizational structure, and the style of management.

Sources and Level of Funding

Well-funded institutions tend to have large endowments, thereby having significant advantages over those with limited resources. Nevertheless, they have certain disadvantages with respect to some IT-related decision making. It is more difficult to gain support for significant leveraging of resources, making it harder to define and implement standards. Faculty and staff are likely to develop and justify unique solutions to IT challenges, which increases the numbers of support personnel, necessitates a greater variety of training, and complicates systems architecture, with a heavier maintenance burden.

Sources of funding have a significant impact on IT policy and practices. Good governance and management depend to some degree on a predictable stream of operational and capital funds. Institutions that must depend heavily on tuition and fees for ongoing funding do not enjoy such predictability. Similarly, state-assisted institutions with little research activity and limited endowments are vulnerable to random occurrences that cause interruptions in the steady flow of funds, which makes planning more difficult.

These factors affect the degree of risk that will be tolerated from governance and decision-making perspectives. That, in turn, affects the type of technology that is selected and supported and the level of service provided.

Leadership Style

The leadership style of the CEO and the executive officers determines many of the parameters for successful governance and decision making. To succeed, the CIO must have insight into the philosophy of all of the executive officers and work to develop processes that fit the particular environment (Zastrocky and Schlier, 2000).

The administrative model of a president with a provost as the chief academic officer may be the most frequently occurring model in mid- to large-sized universities. In research institutions, the most common CIO is a vice provost, followed by a CIO at the vice-presidential level. Many comprehensive universities follow the vice-presidential model as well (Latimer, 2000). In some models, the president or chancellor relies more on someone other than the academic leader. That person might be an executive vice president, the vice president for business and finance, or the primary fundraiser for the institution. In situations where the CIO reports to someone other than the CEO or the academic leader, he or she has difficulty overcoming barriers with faculty and others in the academic arena. In such circumstances, the CIO must be active in the cabinet, or the likelihood of developing a sound governance and decision-making structure is doubtful.

Although often referenced, the model of the president's using an executive team is not widespread in higher education or elsewhere (Katzenbach, 1997). Where it does occur, it provides an ideal environment for a CIO to lead the development of excellent governance and decision-making processes.

Formality of Planning

How an institution conducts planning affects governance and decision making. The formality of that process results in differing amounts of documentation regarding college or university plans. In some colleges and universities, planning is an informal process that results in infrequent production of a document, perhaps every five years, while in others, the process is more formal and more frequent. Whatever the institutional model, IT planning should align with the model so that IT initiatives roll up into the accomplishment of college or university goals and objectives.

A formal planning model can be adapted within an informal atmosphere if the IT governance structure is designed to fit decision-making processes. The CIO, however, must first spend time and energy to sell the concept of formalized IT planning to a critical mass of constituents, including executive officers, which ensures that the process produces results.

Many colleges and universities use a modified home-grown planning process derived by the campus planning administrator or committee rather than an accepted higher education model, such as that of Shirley (1983), Bryson (1995), or Dolence, Rowley, and Lujan (1997). In such cases, documentation exists but is not as extensive as one would find with a formal model. Either a conventional formal IT planning model or an adapted one could be used.

In organizations that do formal planning, the IT planning model is the same as that used by the institution. The plan would be one of several tactical plans that are aligned with and roll up into the institutional strategic plan. It would be developed and refreshed in accord with the defined budget cycle and have a rolling two- to five-year outlook. Most institutional plans are strategic; however, tactical plans have more detail and link operational elements directly with the strategic initiatives and then tie into the budgeting and evaluation processes.

Organizational Culture

The culture of a group is defined as "a pattern of shared basic assumptions that the group learned as it solved its problems of external adaptation and internal integration, that has worked well enough to be considered valid and, therefore, to be taught to new members as the correct way to perceive, think, and feel in relation to those problems" (Schein, 1997, p. 12). This translates into a far stronger pull on the average worker than suggestions or directives from the executive level of an organization. Thus, for most day-to-day activities, culture determines how things get done.

If the institutional culture is one of mistrust and if administrative silos exist, building a good IT governance and decision-making structure will be difficult. The process of establishing needed communication channels will be hard to bring about; even if it is successful initially, the culture will work to subvert them.

Typically, colleges and universities have a collegial organizational culture. The meaning of this varies but to some degree refers to the fact that diverse segments of the campus are involved and have input into decisions that will affect them. In such organizations, it is imperative for the IT governance structure to be representative and for the decision-making processes to be reasonably deliberate, enabling a wide range of IT clients to have some meaningful voice in how their services are provided.

Campuses fortunate enough to have open and trusting organizational cultures have the potential to build solid IT governance and management processes that enable decision making based on the concurrence of a critical mass rather than consensus agreement. More time may then be spent by IT managers and their clients on the questions under consideration rather than in conducting the needed politics or focusing on the care and upkeep of the process so necessary in many environments.

Decision-Making Style of the Executive Officers

Another element that affects organizational culture is the decision-making style of the president or chancellor and her or his cabinet. The cultural impact of decision making may be due to perceptions rather than how things are actually done, but that impact should not be underestimated. Positive perceptions of executive officers may influence cultural change in the long run, whereas negative perceptions immediately reinforce harmful elements in the existing culture.

Highly centralized decision-making structures are usually justified based on efficiencies, and certainly they speed up the process. The lasting effects, however, are not very efficient and are less likely to be effective in a world of both human and technology-based networks and ever increasing communication.

Some CEOs favor a distributed decision-making style with a great deal of independence from one unit to another. Such environments have IT governance and decision-making processes that usually work well for them. Typically, the central IT unit has responsibility for the basic infrastructure and campuswide facilitation of cooperative arrangements. Distributed IT units have autonomy in making local IT decisions and adhere to standards primarily where they have an interface with the basic infrastructure. The most successful institutions of this type are those with considerable resources.

A distributed collegial approach is a prevalent decision-making style of higher education CEOs. Such a method might be characterized as creating a governance structure that encourages input from all affected sectors of the organization and pushes decision making to the level where it can best be made. It seeks to bring leverage across the institution where that makes sense and to delegate to the local level when that is best. The distributed collegial style enables CIOs to work with executive officers to build governance and management processes that can well serve both infrastructure development and service performance.

Type of IT Leadership

A majority of all colleges and universities now have IT leadership positions characterized as CIOs (Green, 2001). The span of responsibility, authority, placement within the organization, and institutional impact varies considerably from institution to institution. The nature of this position significantly affects the success of IT governance and decision-making structures.

CIOs who are executive officers of the institution have great responsibility for both leadership of a major operational unit and institutional policy development. In large universities and research-intensive settings, CIOs often are not executive officers but nevertheless are members of the president's cabinet. Having a seat at the table is the most crucial element for a CIO to be successful in facilitating the development of effective governance and management processes. Cabinet members typically are involved in the breadth of college or university decision making and thus are in an excellent position to facilitate the development of IT governance and decision-making processes that are well aligned and fit the institutional climate and culture.

CIOs who are not members of the president's cabinet do not have advantages that are important in leading the development of governance and decision-making processes successfully. Their ability to gain insight into the inner workings of the executive administration is limited, thereby making it more difficult to align IT and institutional decisions.

Elements of IT Governance

The governance bodies and the role definitions of decision-making groups are keys to processes that further the best use of IT in accomplishing institutional goals and objectives.

Governance Bodies

Different institutional bodies are usually involved in IT governance and decision making. It is very important to define and clarify the roles of the groups and the potential implications of their actions.

An overall IT policy and decision-making body should be defined based on the mixture of institutional characteristics discussed previously in this chapter. It should reflect the makeup of individuals who are strategically involved in institutional decision making. It should be the approval authority for all IT policy and for major IT initiatives. In addition, the members need to be charged with providing support for the implementation of decisions.

Depending on the size and type of institution, advisory committees defined to address specific needs of constituencies can be useful. The nature of their advisory status must be carefully defined. Advisory committee members can usefully provide review duties, participate in evaluation of proposals, populate work teams, and participate in drafting policy recommendations.

IT initiatives often require cross-functional teams for implementation, and often such teams remain in place to support and enhance ongoing system operation. The teams usually consist of staff from functional offices, system clients, and IT staff with responsibilities related to the specific system. Appropriately configured and properly trained cross-functional teams can be highly effective in dealing with the day-to-day complexities of operational systems.

Most campuses have special interest groups that focus on certain software or role-specific systems. They typically meet periodically to discuss related issues and share useful operational information. Incorporating such groups into the governance process can be useful. They may contribute through their detailed operational knowledge of the system and can serve as points of influence in attaining buy-in when upgrades or changes are needed.

Interrelationships of Various IT Groups

The interrelationships of the governance bodies on any campus are extremely important in maintaining good decision making. The same is true of the IT units and IT positions that exist across the institution.

The roles and duties of the various governance councils and committees must be aligned for maximum effectiveness. Typically, the IT policy council is the designated decision-making body. Its focus is on establishing appropriate institution-wide policy, reviewing and authorizing major IT initiatives, approving the IT plan, providing support to remove barriers, and in general focusing on the big picture. Such a group must guard against becoming detailed decision makers, leaving that to designated IT and functional managers. Advisory committees need to understand the advisory role. This is not to say that their input is not meaningful; just the opposite is true. Their perspective must be taken into account when policy is developed and daily operational decisions are made. But they must recognize that final policy decisions come from the policy group and that managers are responsible for daily operational decision making.

In a similar fashion, it is important to align the roles and responsibilities of the various IT units that exist across the campus. The nature of this alignment will vary considerably depending on variables already delineated. The differing roles of central IT and distributed units have been discussed. Whatever the case, the better that unit roles are understood and the closer the various units work together, the more effectively IT-related institutional objectives will be accomplished.

Finally, alignment of the roles and responsibilities of IT positions across the institution is essential. A common IT career ladder enables professionals to grow and move between distributed and centralized IT roles, broadening their perspective and enabling them ultimately to contribute more to the institution. Defining role responsibilities that complement each other enables centralized staff and distributed staff to work effectively without having to resolve turf issues. It also helps central administrators to allocate resources where they are most needed rather than to areas with the greatest political savvy or power.

A Recommended Model for IT Governance

The following general model has been employed effectively at four universities and can be effectively adapted to a variety of circumstances. The institutions were different in size, type, and funding methods, and they had different campuswide planning models, decision-making styles, and organizational cultures. Although the model was similar in all circumstances, it was adapted to fit each unique circumstance; otherwise, it would not have worked.

The Givens: Presidential Understanding and Support

Common to each environment were three factors believed to be fundamental to success. First, the CEO in each situation understood the full importance of IT to all sectors of the institution and understood that changes were needed in the IT organization and decision making for it to be best used. Second, each CEO recruited a CIO with the assurance that significant executive support would be forthcoming. Finally, the CEOs concurred with the concept of using a formal IT planning *and* management model linked to budget and personnel evaluation as a means of initializing the needed changes.

Type of CIO

Each CEO created a cabinet-level CIO position, and each pledged to be personally involved with the CIO in helping to design and implement the IT governance structure to make it fit the environment. The CIO position was clearly defined as fulfilling the IT policy role for the university and as the leader of the institution-wide IT strategic planning process. The CIO was involved in general institutional decision making, not just IT decisions. This is always a key element to success of the CIO.

Definition of Policy and Decision-Making Roles

An IT policy group made up of key decision makers across the campus was developed and given broad responsibility for deriving policy, approving major institutional IT initiatives, approving the IT plan, and making detailed recommendations to the budget committee concerning the allocation of IT resources, both central and distributed. In each situation, this was primary to success. Three IT advisory committees were established: one focused on academic issues, one on administrative issues, and one on student issues. The makeup of each was representative of the defined constituencies. The advisory committees interlocked with the policy body by having chairs of the committees on the policy group. On issues that cut across constituents, each committee gave input.

Definition of Central and Distributed IT Unit Roles

This definition was different on each campus, but in each case, roles were clearly delineated and communicated—required for achieving desired goals. In the most distributed environment, the role of central IT was to focus on the general IT infrastructure, provide support for administrative systems, coordinate school-based academic and research efforts where beneficial, and facilitate the IT planning process to ensure that distributed units were included. In the more universally standardized setting, leveraging hardware and software purchases across all academic and administrative units was stressed. This was done by allowing exceptions to standards only on approval by the CIO, with monitoring performed by central purchasing. In this situation, central IT also carried more responsibility for providing training for distributed staffs. The institutional IT help desk used a centralized database to log calls for assistance, with automated routing to the appropriate central or distributed resource.

Definition of IT Planning Style

The same formal planning model was used in each circumstance, which linked strategic planning with management, tied objectives to allocated budget, and assigned personal responsibilities to managers, thus ensuring that most objectives were completed. In each case, the plan was refreshed annually with a three-year rolling scenario. Needed culture change for the central IT unit was addressed within the model; all distributed IT unit plans were part of the final document; and all segments of the client community were involved in the process before it was finalized (Penrod, 2003). The general methodology was much the same for all institutions, but the who, why, how, and when questions were uniquely answered to fit the overall institutional processes for each campus.

Critical Success Factors

The following elements are critical to success in designing and implementing an IT governance and decision-making structure on any campus:

- Ensure that there is a philosophical fit between the CIO's style of leadership and management and that of the institution's CEO.
- Ensure that the CIO position is at the cabinet level and that the incumbent establishes relationships within the group that enable a level playing field.
- Match the governance structure that is created to the decision-making style of the institution.
- Align the IT plan with institutional planning, and link it to budget, implementation processes, and unit and individual performance.

- Build processes into governance that focus on alignment, and develop mutual trust between all IT units and their clients.

- Carefully develop role definitions, and care for them over time.

- Build varied and continuous feedback loops into the governance, decision-making, and planning processes.

- Assess results from governance and planning, and report them regularly to all IT constituents.

- Remain open to adjusting processes to better fit the environment or to accommodate a changing environment, and have a methodology defined to do so.

- Educate constituents, communicating to them the vision, opportunities for involvement, annual objectives, and results.

Conclusion

Building and maintaining an IT governance structure of any kind is not easy; to design and implement one as complex as that described in this chapter is indeed difficult. If it is successful, it is primarily for two reasons: it produces reliable results for clients, and it saves time and effort otherwise spent elsewhere in the IT organization. Whatever the methodology, the objective must be to improve services to clients and support institutional mission and goals.

References

Bryson, J. M. *Strategic Planning for Public and Nonprofit Organizations*. (Rev. ed.) San Francisco: Jossey-Bass, 1995.

Dolence, M. G., Rowley, D. J., and Lujan, H. D. *Working Toward Strategic Change*. San Francisco: Jossey-Bass, 1997.

Green, K. C. *Campus Computing 2001: The Twelfth National Survey of Computing and Information Technology in American Higher Education*. Encino, Calif.: Campus Computing Project, 2001.

Katzenbach, J. R. "The Myth of the Top Management Team." *Harvard Business Review*, Nov.–Dec. 1997, pp. 82–91.

Latimer, D. "A National Study of Chief Information Officers in U.S. Higher Education." [www.CIOsInAcademia.org]. 2000.

Penrod, J. I. "Creating a Realistic IT Vision." *Technology Source*, March–April 2003. [ts.mivu.org].

Schein, E. H. *Organizational Culture and Leadership*. (2nd ed.) San Francisco: Jossey-Bass, 1997.

Shirley, R. C. "Identifying the Levels of Strategy for a College or University." *Long Range Planning*, 1983, *16*(3), 92–98.

Zastrocky, M. R., and Schlier, F. "The Higher Education CIO in the Twenty-First Century." *EDUCAUSE Quarterly*, 2000, *23*(1), 53, 59. [www.educause.edu/ir/library/pdf/eq/a001/eqm0018.pdf].

3

Organizing Information Resources for Effective Management

James G. Neal, Polley Ann McClure

Individuals and groups of people carry out roles and work together to achieve shared objectives within a formal social structure and with established processes. This is the basic definition of an organization. In this chapter, we seek to stimulate awareness and understanding about the current status, diversity, and future development of information resources (IR) organizational structures in colleges and universities. We address the nature and purpose of organizational structures in general, consider organization in the context of the higher education culture, recommend six general principles for designing effective higher education IR organizations and examine how myriad factors will influence choice of IR organizational design, and suggest some developments that may have implications for IR organizational structures and processes in the future.

The Nature and Purpose of Structure

Organizations have been a subject of analysis and critique in the management literature, and the processes of organizational design

We appreciate the contributions of Gary Augustson, Pennsylvania State University; Elliott Shore, Bryn Mawr College; and Norma Holland, Indiana University, to our descriptions of the information technology organizations at their institutions.

and development have been documented in both theoretical and research presentations. Organizational structures define relationships and roles and the systems through which goals and priorities are established, decisions are made, resources are allocated, power is wielded, and plans are accomplished. They determine the degree to which administrative responsibility and authority are distributed and shared, operations and procedures are integrated and flexible, and policies and standards are designed and enforced. Organizational fluidity and vitality are important factors in productivity and success.

Organization theory looks at a variety of parameters to define organizational models, with particular focuses on these:

- Centralization and decentralization
- Hierarchy and adhocracy
- Bureaucracy and distribution
- Simplicity and complexity
- Formality and informality
- Administration and entrepreneurship
- Authority and collaboration

Organizations can be viewed, among many characteristics, in terms of layers and rigidity of structure, direction and effectiveness of information flow, sources and impact of leadership, participation in decision making, freedom of action, and levels of ambiguity. Particularly important are the environmental conditions that can influence organizational design, including the health of an industry, the level of competition, the speed of technological change, the extent of globalization, the degree of professionalization in the field, and the rapidity of new knowledge creation. This summary exploration of organizational characteristics itself reflects the broad range of perspectives and the labyrinth of traits and trends that affect structure and process.

Organizational Models in Higher Education

The higher education community, often described as poorly run but highly effective, presents a unique organizational tradition. Even as colleges and universities have grown in size and complexity, the historical dualism that brings together a conventional administrative hierarchy with the networked structure associated with academic governance and faculty decision making has been preserved.

Information resources organizations have grown up in this two-headed beast, and even today and in the most completely integrated organizations, the vestiges of this history are easily seen. IR organizations whose leadership is rooted on the academic side of the institution often exhibit structures and styles that are more akin to those of faculty departments than they are like the hierarchical business organizations they report to.

Colleges and universities have struggled to distribute authority, integrate key operations, break down bureaucratic processes, achieve less rigidity in structure, promote more cooperation across units, and build more matrix-type approaches to the work of the institution. Higher education has had strong flirtations with such initiatives as Total Quality Management, reengineering, and the learning organization, but little has been fundamentally changed in the traditional system-driven management models and the complex and conventional administrative hierarchies.

It is questionable whether higher education should or could effectively integrate the structures and strategies of the corporate environment and whether new management models can easily map into the classic academic bureaucracy. Not only is there often lack of clarity in institutional mission and goals, but they also are often multiple and conflicting. As a result, centralized planning and resource allocation systems often coexist with broadly distributed and loosely coupled structures across academic divisions and with an expanding array of maverick organizations like research centers and entrepreneurial enterprises. The independence of faculty as teachers and investigators and their collective control over the principal products of the institution, that is, learning and new knowledge, add an often unfathomable and schizophrenic character to the organizational culture of higher education.

An inventory of the types of functions that exist within most colleges and universities under the umbrella of information resources and technology demonstrates the breadth and depth of the enterprise. These can include administrative computing, academic and research computing, networks, telephony, student computing, instructional technology, libraries, media services, language laboratories, print services, computer stores, mailrooms, Web support services, and electronic publishing.

Principles for Organizing Information Resources

Because institutions of higher education span the spectrum from small (both in enrollment and geography), relatively focused liberal arts colleges to large, spread-out, and highly diverse research universities—not to mention the spectrum of private to public to for-profit funding, single campus to multicampus system, and associate degree to doctoral granting—it is not surprising that the models for organizing the IR function are also highly diverse. Nevertheless, there are some general principles that may be of use in thinking about individual situations.

Establish a Locus of Institutional Responsibility

Regardless of the point on the range of diversity described above, one general organizational issue is where to place the institutional responsibility for the IR functions. A decade ago, responsibility for IR, even central IR functions, was distributed among senior executives. Today, most institutions have recognized the need for high-level leadership with broad responsibility for coordination across the institution (Green, 2001). Specific titles vary, but these positions are often referred to, formally or informally, as chief information officers, or CIOs.

Most CIOs report to the president or chancellor, the provost, or the administrative vice president or chief financial officer (Penrod, Chapter Two, this volume). They are often members of the executive staff and participate in important institutional decisions. However, even when they occupy these strategic roles, they rarely have direct management responsibility for all of the IR-related functions in the diverse and decentralized research university. They may not have direct responsibility for distributed support units within colleges and departments or for the libraries. Commonly, they will have direct responsibility for the centrally provided communications services, administrative data services, and general institutional services such as e-mail and calendaring. Depending on local priorities, they may have responsibility for high-performance computing and instructional and classroom technologies. Green (2001) and Latimer (2000) provide analyses of the functions normally included in the CIO portfolio. The examples of IR organizations that follow illustrate the variations that exist among institutions.

Bryn Mawr College

The CIO at Bryn Mawr, a progressive small liberal arts institution, has comprehensive responsibility for all of the IR elements, including libraries and distributed support. This college has developed a highly original structure in which library and academic computing staff are deployed around the campus in discipline-focused clusters (science, humanities, and so forth). Faculty coordinators help to ensure that local priorities govern support activities, but the staff still report to the institutional IR organization to ensure coordination, professional development, and standards.

Columbia University

This large urban undergraduate and graduate university with a strong research focus was an early integrator of information technology (IT) functions under a single administrator. By the early 1970s, all computing and telecommunications areas were administered by a CIO, reporting to the executive vice president for academic affairs. In 1986, this structure was expanded to include the university libraries. By 1989, the pendulum had swung back in the other direction, with administrative computing and telephone services moving to report to an administrative vice president. Academic computing, network services, and the libraries continued to report to a university librarian who was also a vice president, and this unit has now been expanded to include an electronic publishing group, an electronic pedagogy group, and a center for digital library research and development. Several large professional schools and academic departments have developed resident IT support staff who work in varying degrees of coordination with the central administrative and academic computing organizations.

The Pennsylvania State University

Penn State is probably unique among higher education institutions in having twenty-four campuses that are geographically distributed yet function as part of a single university. The CIO has academic computing, administrative computing, telecommunications, and IT security reporting to his office. The libraries are outside the CIO responsibility, although the CIO organization does run the library systems and has a close working relationship with the dean of libraries. IT support staff on distributed campuses report to their campus administrations, but work closely with the CIO's organization to ensure coordination. On the University Park campus, many units have local IT support staff who are in close communication with the central organization.

Indiana University

IU, also a large multicampus institution, appointed a vice president for IT and CIO (VPIT/CIO) in 1997 with direct responsibility for a multicampus organization of over twelve hundred staff members who deliver IT services on the two core campuses, located in Bloomington and Indianapolis. In addition, the main IT organization coordinates local support and services at six other campuses through campus CIOs, who report jointly to the VPIT/CIO and campus chancellor. The libraries at all eight campuses are also part of a fairly centralized structure, reporting to the university librarian, and they work in collaboration with the IT organization on numerous initiatives. Local IT support personnel in departments and schools throughout the university, although not formally part of the central IT organization, collaborate and coordinate with service delivery units within University Information Technology Services.

Define Roles and Responsibilities Clearly

Once a decision is made about the nature and locus of institutional responsibility for information resources, it is important to define the extent and limits of the institutional role and, by inference, the extent and limits of the roles of other managers within the institution. For example, if the first decision is that there will be a CIO with certain functions reporting to that office, the second set of decisions should address the other IR functions that are not part of the CIO office and how their roles relate to the CIO office and to each other. This is clearly important when the library does not report to the CIO, but it is also important for all the other central units, like printing and media services, as well as the distributed support units. What is the relationship between the desktop support and local area network administrators within departments and the central network and computing support organization?

Formally Organize Distributed Support

It is often the case that executives thinking about organizing IR on campus focus exclusively on structure for the central IR organizations. In complex research universities, the majority of IR staff are outside the central organizations and are often not effectively part of any IR organization.

The president or provost and CIO should work directly with deans and other vice presidents to suggest organizational structures for use within their units that can improve service and efficiency and facilitate coordination across the whole institution. For example, it is very common to find that single IT support persons with responsibility for individual departments or buildings report to departmental administrative assistants or assistant chairpersons. These individuals have no backup and, in many cases, no effective supervision. Although the protocols and conventions they deploy might be effective as long as the specific individual is there to maintain them, they often are completely unsupportable in the absence of their creator.

Schools or colleges should organize the general IR support people at the level of the school or college and then assign them to a primary department, building, or disciplinary group. By making them part of a larger IR support organization, someone can cross-train them, arrange to have them cover for each other, and develop some standards and conventions. The manager of this college- or school-based unit could have informal managerial responsibility to someone in the central IR department for purposes of institution-wide coordination.

Most large and complex institutions agree that it is important to have IR support staff working within departments close to the people they support, but the lack of coordination can significantly increase the cost. McClure, Smith, and Lockard (1999) and Miller (2002) provide extended analysis of structures and mechanisms for organizing distributed IT support.

Recognize That Structures Often Depend on the People Available

Especially at the institutional level, the availability of individuals with the content and leadership skills for specific roles will be a major determinant of the structure selected. If there is a person in whom the chief executive and the rest of the institution have confidence for a particular role, it is much easier to design a structure to support the person and role than if there is disagreement or competitive claims on the role. It is not uncommon to have executive leadership break up an integrated IT or IR organization when the strong leader who held them together leaves the institution. Executives need to be conscious of this dynamic because the rhetoric characterizing these decisions does not always clarify whether the rationale is one of objective structure or key person dependency. Either is a valid consideration; what is important is to understand which is driving the decision.

Use Common Sense

If you combine people into a single organization, their purposes are more likely to harmonize and converge than not. If you put them into separate structures, their work will diverge. So thinking about organization structure involves identifying the most important dimension of the institution to have coherence on the IR front and then organizing accordingly.

For example, you could decide that having IR support the specific unique academic programs of the institution is the most important goal. That would suggest assigning the IR staff to schools and colleges and perhaps not even having a central academic computing or library function. This arrangement would probably not be the most cost-effective organization, nor would it produce a technological or information infrastructure that has coherence at the institution-wide level. Also, because leadership ability and deep technical skills are generally in limited supply, the institution might find itself falling behind its institutional peers, unable to keep pace with technological change and limited in its ability to advance its mission through technology.

As another example, if you decide that having common administrative processes across the entire institution is most important, that would suggest aligning administrative computing to the core functional administrative units centrally. This arrangement would probably not produce an information infrastructure that ideally meets the desires of the distributed departments, however, and they would likely create shadow systems.

These examples illustrate the concept that the organization of the IR function is a strategic issue and should be determined by the strategic priorities of the institution.

Design Organizations to Enable Them to Change

With the underlying technologies changing so rapidly and the institutional priorities and needs also evolving, perhaps the most important principle to the design of IR organizations is that the structures should support and enable change. When the technologies supporting audiovisual, high-performance computing, and accounting processing, for example, were all unique and incompatible, separate and independent organizations supported them. As these and other functions came to be based on common platforms, the need for separate organizations vanished, and campuses reorganized accordingly.

IR organizations are among the most dynamic on campus. This need for organizational change is met in some institutions through frequent reorganization, an approach that is very hard on the IR staff, who have little continuity in relationships and priorities. It is also hard on the customers, patrons, and other users of their services. They complain that they never know where to go to find the support they need. A different approach is to build a more classical functional base organization and to draw individuals from this persistent structure to create short-lived project teams to accomplish specific purposes. Savage (1990) and Hastings (1993) describe some of the benefits and the challenges of creating and managing such an organization.

In our experience, the greatest challenge is in developing the IR staff's abilities to function in the matrix-like structure, where they are accountable to both a project manager and a line manager. The managers have to learn how to develop processes designed to resolve the inevitable conflicts among themselves.

Factors Affecting Structure and Process

Institutional characteristics that influence some of the important differences in IR organizational infrastructure include size, control (private versus public), scope of research mission, single versus multicampus structure, presence of professional schools, funding, planning traditions, faculty governance, and tolerance for risk. Another important factor is leadership, that is, the vision and involvement of academic administrators, IR managers, and faculty in pushing the IR agenda and recognizing the link between organizational development and advancement and success. (See the related discussion in Chapter Two.)

It is also important to consider the relationship of technology adoption and integration to organizational development, in that the deeper IR is integrated into administrative systems and academic lifestyles, the more robust and central the IR structure and process become. Importance leads to attention, which leads to action in the academy.

Organizational structure has an important impact on several key aspects of organizational process and character:

- IR organizations often bring together units with very different cultural traditions (the customary beliefs, social norms, styles, thought patterns, and behaviors that characterize a group of people). An administrative computing group coming out of a mainframe or a fee-for-service tradition looks at IR very differently than does an academic computing group coming out of a faculty-based and more free-wheeling tradition or a library group that has centuries rather than decades of professional development and is struggling also to manage large legacy responsibilities. They think differently, they value different things, they work together in different ways, they look at relationships differently, and they relate to the academic culture with remarkable diversity.

- IR organizations often bring together units with very different approaches to leadership (the capacity for vision, guidance, and influence) and power (the ability to control, motivate, influence, and exercise authority). An administrative tradition would suggest a more hierarchical and bureaucratic style with clear lines of authority and the linking of power to decision making. An academic tradition would suggest a more deliberative and consultative style with the linking of power to process and distribution of responsibility. The effective coexistence or integration of these different routines is an important challenge in higher education.

- IR organizations often bring together units with very different understandings of strategy development (the actions that make an organization more competitive and successful) and planning (the process of evaluating options and establishing goals and priorities). Again, an administrative tradition would point to a stronger commitment to strategic process, and an academic tradition would point to a fuzzier and less business-like manner.

- IR organizations often bring together units with very different communication and collaboration practices. By communication, we mean the exchange or sharing of information through common systems of symbols and behaviors, and by collaboration, we mean cooperation and working together across organizational boundaries. The dynamics of technological change and the increasing centrality of technology to higher education success argue for a more deliberative and consistent commitment to effective communication and collaboration. The degree to which oral, written, or electronic communication traditions predominate and coexist, and the extent to which there is openness to working with others from different backgrounds and with conflicting priorities, will be critical to the effective evolution of IR organizational development.

- IR organizations often bring together units with different views on budgeting and resource allocation, that is, the administration of available funds and the assignment of organizational assets to different activities. In higher education, some IR units have been

funded out of institutional resources through the central administrative budget or through some formula-based allocation of costs to
units that consume IR services. In other cases, IR units have been
expected to charge for services and to operate on a subsidized or
cost-recovery basis. And in other cases, IR units have been charged
with generating new resources from outside the institution, perhaps
through obtaining grants, fundraising, or the development of products and services for new markets. (Chapter Four elaborates on
these concepts.)

• IR organizations often bring together units with different
views on assessment, that is, the determination of the value, importance, and impact of a program or a service. All higher education
institutions are increasingly under expanded scrutiny and accountability from boards, legislatures, and students, and this scrutiny
touches IR organizations very directly. There are no clear measures
of return on investment for IR or of the impact on the quality and
reputation of the institution. Administrative computing traditions
may be more focused on quantitative measures, and academic computing may be more comfortable with qualitative studies. Libraries
historically have been evaluated through input measures, while
there are clear expectations for more documentation of output assessment. (See the discussion of assessment in Chapter Nine.)

The central issue in the consideration of these various issues is
the meaning of "bring together" and the extent to which the various
IR units work in a college or university independently, collaboratively, administratively linked, or organizationally integrated. The
degree of integration will highlight the different traditions and practices, the compatibility of cultures, the effectiveness of leadership
and planning, the quality of communication and cooperation, the
rigor of resource allocation, and the impact of assessment across
newly coupled IR units.

Bringing these differentiated perspectives together in a merged
organization can be an enormously powerful way to evoke the active

and creative rethinking of the underlying issues. Separate organizations that have been allowed to harden into polarized positions sometimes can find common ground only through consolidation and the associated requirement to sort out a new shared view on all of these things.

The Implications of Future IR Development

Just as higher education technological developments have influenced campus IR organizations in the past, we believe that many such developments on the horizon will have implications for IR structure and process in the future, including the following:

- Expanded growth of national and global network capacity and performance to meet the demands of scientific and research computing and new high-demand applications

- Increased importance of improved IR security and disaster preparedness

- A desire to deploy new portal services in both the administrative and academic arenas

- Enterprise-wide system implementations to manage administrative functions and services

- New national information policies in such areas as privacy, intellectual property, and intellectual freedom

- Implementation of institutional repositories and asset management systems to capture and manage the digital assets of a college or university

- New initiatives in on-line publishing and on-line course development pushed out to external markets

- Massive conversion of print to electronic resources in library collections

- Personal digital assistant device technology

- Broad-based electronic records management systems to archive institutional information

- Cross-institutional approaches to preservation of the scholarly record and to sharing of IR expertise

Conclusion

There is no single recipe for the one right way to organize the IR function within higher education institutions. There are, however, some basic guidelines that can help with the design process. First, we suggest that the ability of the organization to evolve gracefully to meet the incessant change that will buffet it be given very heavy weight in the design process. Second, we acknowledge the overarching importance of the availability of persons with the professional and leadership ability to match the challenges facing the institution. It makes no sense to design an organization for a fully integrated IR structure if the institution does not have and is unsuccessful at attracting a capable CIO to lead that organization. Finally, whatever the structure, it should be consonant with the overall structure and culture of the institution it is to serve, and it should attempt to define structure, roles, and responsibilities throughout the enterprise, not just in the central offices.

References

Green, K. C. *Campus Computing 2001: The Twelfth National Survey of Computing and Information Technology in American Higher Education.* Encino, Calif.: Campus Computing Project, 2001.

Hastings, C. *The New Organization.* Berkshire, England: McGraw-Hill International, 1993.

Latimer, D. "A National Study of Chief Information Officers in U.S. Higher Education." [www.CIOsInAcademia.org]. 2000.

McClure, P. A., Smith, J. W., and Lockard, T. W. "Distributed Computing Support." In D. G. Oblinger and R. N. Katz (eds.), *Renewing Administration: Preparing Colleges and Universities for the Twenty-First Century.* Bolton, Mass.: Anker, 1999.

Miller, F. "Organizing Information Professionals on Campus." *EDUCAUSE Quarterly,* 2002, 25(4), 46-51. [www.educause.edu/ir/library/pdf/eqm0247.pdf.]

Savage, C. M. *Fifth Generation Management.* Bedford, Mass.: Digital Press, 1990.

4

Getting Beyond Budget Dust to Sustainable Models for Funding Information Technology

David L. Smallen, Jack McCredie

Today's students and faculty expect—and demand—world-class access to electronic information technology (IT). At the core of a modern college or university IT infrastructure is its communications network and the literally millions of servers connected to it on campus and throughout the rest of the world, with associated applications, data resources, services, and on-line communities of colleagues. How to pay for these resources while providing the maximum benefit for the institution is the question explored in this chapter.

Generating adequate resources is a challenge because the use of IT in higher education has matured greatly in the past few decades, and IT expenditures are increasing faster than general operating budgets at many institutions. In 2001–2002, for example, the median per capita increase in IT budgets for the schools that participated in the COSTS project[1] was 11 percent (Smallen and Leach, 2002). Which funding models will provide the sustainable foundation on which colleges and universities can build the information resource infrastructure they need?

Budget dust is a term sometimes used to describe the unplanned temporary budget surpluses that in good years remain unexpended at the close of fiscal accounting periods. In this chapter, we use the term more broadly to mean temporary funds from any source that are not expected to be available on an ongoing basis. Many IT organizations have depended on these unpredictable windfalls as the primary source of funding for new initiatives or as a substitute for sustainable funding strategies.

IT organizations cannot thrive, or even remain viable, on budget dust. They need a scalable, long-term funding strategy that derives directly from the strategic objectives of the institution. This strategy must fit the campus management culture and its priorities, while encouraging efficient use of IT resources. We know of no single formula or template that fits the needs of all institutions. However, several common building blocks have been successful at many campuses.

Each institution needs to develop its own customized long-term IT funding strategy, which will most likely be a blend of these basic components. In this chapter, we outline several goals that should serve as guiding principles for this design process. We then describe a few key strategies and funding mechanisms that are common in higher education. We close with some cautions for those who are developing funding strategies.

Design Principles

We recommend the design principles discussed in the following sections for developing sustainable IT funding processes.

Align IT Resources with Institutional Priorities

A successful funding model must ensure that technology infrastructure and services are able to support institutional priorities. For example, if a college or university encourages faculty to use technology to enhance the learning experience, the revenue stream for replacing desktop computers must be sufficient so that faculty who use technology in their courses can continue to use the latest versions of software and adequate hardware. Funding for technology should also take into account whether the campus leaders want the campus to be a pioneer, close follower, middle of the pack, or trailing institution with respect to the application of technology to its core processes.

Integrate IT with the Management Culture

IT is a strategic resource, and management at all levels should consider its priorities at the same time, and in similar ways, as it evaluates other strategic campus needs. If the campus must make a trade-off between a new wing on a building and a wireless network, for example, the same group should be setting priorities for both matters.

Promote Efficient Use of Institutional Resources

Charging for telephone services encourages people to find the least expensive way of making calls, for example, during evenings and weekends. Charging a monthly fee for each network access point can encourage departments to make wise choices about the location of network outlets. It is important to recognize that the time it takes people to accomplish a task is a valuable resource. Centralized laser printing might save on the cost of laser printers but cost extra time as users trundle back and forth to the printer.

Support Institutional Technology Standards

To create a supportable and sustainable IT environment, the institution should promote standards to ensure interoperability of computer systems. Some organizations are developing well-planned campuswide IT architectures, and the IT funding process should support these designs. Selecting, reviewing, and managing preferred vendors for servers, desktop computers, and generic software (for example, word processing, spreadsheet, and presentation) simplifies technology support, often results in volume purchasing discounts, and encourages competition. Many institutions have centralized purchasing guidelines that encourage conformity to standards. Others provide incentives through discounts to achieve adherence to standards. Note, however, that research activities often require non-standard products.

Promote Effective Management of IT Resources

Issues such as security, reliability, and the quality and accuracy of information are central to managing IT resources effectively. Although general operating budgets may be allocated on a yearly basis, having multiyear fiscal plans and budgets for significant projects promotes stability and effective longer-term management strategies.

When possible, special mechanisms should be in place to encourage innovative uses of technology throughout an organization. Good ideas spring up in the most unlikely places, and small grants or incentive funds as part of the yearly budget cycle can pay large dividends.

Facilitate Generation of Additional Resources for IT

Colleges and universities have multiple income sources. Some IT charging processes make it feasible to tap more than one of these income streams, and others make it more difficult. For example, if a particular service, such as e-mail, is provided at no charge to the general campus community, most government research grants cannot be charged directly for this service since it is free for general users. In addition, some agencies and foundations will not support full overhead charges but will pay directly for services used in grants and contracts.

Ensure Reasonable Transaction Costs for Funding Mechanisms

Billing expenses can become a major cost component for an IT service. For example, telephone companies spend significant resources processing the information required to render a monthly bill. Some funding models are just too complex and too expensive to implement. When faced with this situation, many organizations develop bulk rates for general classes of service rather than detailed usage charges. For example, most retail Internet service providers, including colleges and universities, charge a single monthly fee that is independent of how many times the customer dials into the service or how many bytes are transferred.

Build a Fair and Equitable Funding Process

If users believe that a funding or budgeting process is fair and equitable, they will cooperate with it. If they believe that it is arbitrary or pernicious, they will find ways to subvert it. The current confused and unworkable state of copyright regulations with respect to Internet use of materials is an illustration. Until the music industry invents a way of charging for products that its customers believe is fair and equitable, we will continue to see widescale violations of copyright, bitter conflicts, and unworkable regulations.

Strategies and Building Blocks

We consider here three primary sources of revenue for a college or university IT organization and four primary ways of obtaining funds from customers who control these funds. These sources must cover the full costs of the IT operation in one way or another.

Sources of Revenue

The first, and most common, revenue source is general operating funds. This type of funding usually comes from the same source that supports faculty and staff salaries, the library, other academic services, and general campus operations.

A second source of IT funding is grants, contracts, and gifts. Government agencies, corporations, foundations, and individual benefactors provide these resources, usually on a restricted basis for specific activities, initiatives, and projects. The IT organization can be the direct recipient of such funding or a secondary recipient. In the first case, the IT organization is completely responsible for the project. In the second case, an individual researcher or another department gets the contract or grant and subcontracts work to the IT organization. Another way of generating funds from external organizations is through general campus overhead charges applied against contracts, grants, and gifts.

A third source of IT funding is direct charges to individuals who use personal resources and to certain types of departments (for example, auxiliary services such as residential housing and parking) that pay directly for support services. Examples include telecommunications services to students in residence halls or apartments; computers, software, maintenance, and services purchased at campus technology stores; charges for remote access to the campus network; and technology fees charged to individual students. Most often these goods and services are available only to members of the campus community because of restrictions placed on the college or university.

Each of these three types of funding arrangements invites a different kind of input into decisions about the scale, variety, and beneficiaries of IT resources. As long as the IT organization pays attention to the needs of the group that is willing to pay, each funding arrangement can provide information from a different perspective.

Models for Funding

To serve the needs of the broadest range of customers, the IT organization should have flexible charging models for services that fit the needs of the individuals who control these different funding sources. Again for simplicity, we limit our discussion to four fundamental models: centrally funded, usage based, taxed based, and combinations of the other three.

Centrally Funded Model

The centrally funded model (often called the *library model* because library services have traditionally been funded in this manner) assumes that the service is fully paid for by the institution directly through the operating budget of the IT department. The central administration, representing the campus community, is the primary customer, and users of a centrally funded service are not charged for their usage. This creates a need for some administrative mechanism to determine which services will be provided and who gets how much of a particular service. Advisory committees often provide guidance on these decisions.

This is the most common approach for allocating general operating funds. It is frequently used in institutions with strong centralized decision-making processes. Many organizations use this method for activities that provide core services to wide audiences with relatively minor usage-dependent costs and in cases where the institution has an explicit strategy of encouraging access to specific resources. Illustrative services often include e-mail, Web-based course management applications, course-related computing facilities, public access workstations, and base-level network access.

A centrally funded model has the following advantages:

- *Conformity with organizational goals*. Core values and institutional goals are most easily promoted by centrally funding IT services that support these ideals.

- *Uniformity of services*. It is easier to ensure a consistent level of service for centrally funded IT initiatives than it is for services that depend on different departmental revenue streams. For example, at Hamilton College, the replacement of desktop hardware and software, network servers and electronics, and data projectors is funded centrally to ensure a consistent, supportable level of services.

- *Ease of enforcing standards*. Central funding can provide the carrot that enhances, or enforces, standardization.

- *Ease of embarking on new initiatives*. The most expeditious way to move forward on a new initiative is to fund it centrally.

A centrally funded model has the following disadvantages:

- *Difficulty balancing supply and demand.* Without accurate market feedback, it is very difficult to judge what the appropriate budget for a service should be.

- *Difficulty stopping services.* Users soon view centrally funded services as entitlements. With the growth in use of the Internet, institutions that provide centrally funded modem pools find it difficult to maintain service quality. At the same time, users of the service view it as an entitlement and are loathe to switch to a commercial Internet service provider.

- *Difficulty in measuring the value of competing services.* It is very hard to determine the value of support services from the administrative center of a complex organization without market feedback.

Usage-Based Model

Usage charges can equitably recover some or all of the cost of a service with those using more of the service paying more of the cost of providing it. Basic economic logic says that as long as we live in a world of scarcity, it is a waste of resources to produce services for which consumers will not pay. The test of need comes by setting price equal to the marginal cost of producing more service and seeing what happens. Such usage charges have two benefits: they discourage truly frivolous uses while providing valid feedback about whether service needs to be cut back or expanded. After all, if a shortage exists when the usage charge equals marginal cost, then surely more service should be produced until no more can be sold at a price that covers marginal cost.

The case of IT may be a bit complicated, however. IT has many of the properties of a business that produces joint products—such as milk and cream—in which it is the sum of disparate consumers' payments that should cover the marginal cost of the service. More-over, it must be possible to divide the service into controllable units (for example, cost per minute of a telephone call or rent per year for a building).

Examples of areas in which colleges and universities commonly apply direct charges are voice telephony and goods and services supplied from a campus technology store, including hardware support, application development, network connections and services, desktop support, and printing.

A usage-based model has the following advantages:

- *Information and income from charging for services.* Charging for a service provides valuable information about the need for that service while at the same time providing mechanisms to pay for the service and to discourage frivolous usage. For example, central IT organizations often charge hourly rates to provide system administration services for departments or to recover costs of "excess" data storage.

- *Generation of additional income.* A robust charging structure enables an IT organization to charge customers for the IT resources they use.

- *Information to measure success.* A usage-based system generates considerable information that can be used to inform decision making.

A usage-based model has the following disadvantages:

- *Hard-to-achieve strategic objectives.* Decentralized decisions made by independent departments and individuals will not necessarily be in alignment with strategic institutional objectives.

- *Difficulty ensuring equal access.* Ensuring equal access to core IT services requires complex subsidies.

- *High overhead.* Usage-based models require significant administrative overhead.

Tax-Based Model

In tax-based IT funding mechanisms, a specific group that will benefit from a service is identified, and individuals are charged a fee, or tax, because of their membership in the group regardless of how much they consume. The most common example of this approach is the student technology fee used by many colleges and universities, with the typical model being a course-based or term-based fee (Mallette, 2002). To allocate several administrative costs, not just IT expenses, Duke University uses a comprehensive allocation methodology based on the number of people in various units. Another example of a tax-based approach is the process of adding a monthly fixed charge to telephone bills to cover data networking expenses.

A tax-based model has the following advantages:

- *Ease of explanation, implementation, and maintenance.* Tax-based models are much easier to manage and maintain than usage-based systems.

- *Generation of incremental resources.* To the extent that the tax applies to students, the revenue generated is incremental to the general operating budget of the campus.

A tax-based model has the following disadvantages:

- *Opposition to fees.* There may be substantial opposition to the fee, especially among those who use the service less than the average, or not at all, and feel they are taxed unfairly.

- *Scalability.* It is often difficult to generate the funding required to increase the scale of a successful service.

- *Need to demonstrate results.* If a tax-based fee is adver-
  tised to support a specific service, specific results related
  to that service must be quickly demonstrated.

Mixed Models: Blends of the Basic Building Blocks

Many managers discover that a combination of the basic funding
mechanisms produces the most appropriate design for a particular
campus. Variables such as size, management culture, amount of
research volume, current level of IT expenditure, type of IT service,
and history combine and interact in complex ways on every campus. What seems completely natural in one environment may not
work in another. On many campuses, some services (like voice
telephone and the technology store) operate in full cost-recovery
charging mode, while services like basic e-mail and course-related
computing are fully paid for by the central administration.

    Another common mixture is to use different models to support
a single service. The common form of this mechanism is for the administration to fund centrally a substantial fixed cost (like space,
utility charges, or the core campus backbone network) and then for
the IT organization to charge users directly for the marginal costs of
their use. An interesting example of this approach is the scalable
network funding model developed at the University of California,
Berkeley (see cns-pao.berkeley.edu/netfunding/). The central administration pays for the campus backbone and base-level services for
academic departments such as Internet connectivity and building
wiring. Departments must pay for future incremental growth in these
services and for unique advanced service requirements.

    A major advantage of using a blend of models is that the over-
all process can fit well with the culture of the institution. A dis-
advantage is that the resulting process is complex, and users are
often confused as to why certain services are fully or partially funded
centrally while others are priced at market rates. The reality is that
most management processes in higher education evolve slowly.
Rarely do we have an opportunity to design with a clean slate. Of

course, mixed models carry with them some of the advantages and disadvantages of each of the components. The goal is to develop a funding process that will ensure a consistently high level of IT services for the campus.

Six Sure Ways to Fail

Experience shows that despite the best of intentions, many management teams repeatedly make similar mistakes as they strive to build a strong IT function and implement new projects. We now turn to a discussion of the most common of these pitfalls.

Starting Long-Term Projects Without Funding

A common practice is to solicit grant or vendor funding for a developing infrastructure without having a strategy for the long-term maintenance, support, or replacement of these services. The publicity surrounding the creation of a new state-of-the-art computer laboratory fades away, to be replaced by outdated equipment and disappointed faculty and students. The old saying "Be wary of gifts that eat" is appropriate in this context.

Equally common is the practice of beginning a new IT initiative with "budget dust" and hoping for long-term funding after demonstrating the project's success. In good years or up cycles, this strategy often works. However, in down cycles it causes significant problems. Decaying infrastructure, overworked staff, and disillusioned users can be the result.

Focusing on Implementation and Neglecting Ongoing Expenses

Underestimating the full life-cycle costs of a project is a way of unintentionally initiating a project without adequate long-term funding. Even if the project is successful, the budget officer will be unhappy. The best way to avoid this pitfall is to get good advice from colleagues who have completed similar projects. Be wary of cost figures from vendors that are selling a solution. If you are an early adopter of a new service, build in a significant contingency fund at the beginning.

Charging for a Service That Was Once Free

If you intend to charge for a service in the long term, begin charging as early as possible. Taking away a perceived entitlement is much harder than adjusting a price or modifying the form of a charging mechanism that has already been in place.

Using a Secretive Top-Down Planning Approach

In higher education, process is paramount. Involving the user community in the development of a funding model will result in a more acceptable result, as well as widespread understanding of the costs of supporting technology investments. Both are important for successful implementation. The significant up-front investment in education and persuasion is worth the time, although your patience may be stretched to the limit.

Neglecting to Test Funding Assumptions

A common implementation practice is to develop a prototype to test the feasibility of an innovative IT application or service. If you choose this route, do not forget to develop a long-term funding model as part of the pilot project. Having an appropriate funding mechanism is a key ingredient for the success of most projects. Early in the process, begin developing a model that has the capability of scaling with the expansion of the service.

Being Rigid

Developing appropriate IT funding models remains more of an art than a science. Recognize the value of retaining flexibility while experimenting with different funding models. Be careful, but not timid, in trying different approaches when you do not get it exactly right the first time.

Conclusion

Having a solid, well-designed set of funding mechanisms in place enables IT managers to plan for and execute longer-range plans and strategies than would be possible in an environment where funding new initiatives depends on budget dust. Today's high-priority challenges such as recruitment and retention of valuable employees, system and network security, wireless initiatives, high-performance networking, enterprise-level administrative initiatives, course management systems, portals, and general e-strategies to help transform the campus all depend on creative funding processes that will provide long-term support for these initiatives. Developing an appropriate funding model to support an IT initiative may be as important to its long-range success as the quality of the implementation.

Note

1. The Cost of Supporting Technology Services (COSTS) project is an international effort to help leaders in higher education understand their IT investments and staffing levels through the use of benchmarks.

References

Mallette, B. *Student Technology Fees*. Boulder, Colo.: EDUCAUSE, 2002.
Smallen, D., and Leach, K. "Seven Benchmarks for Information Technology Investments." *EDUCAUSE Quarterly*, 2002, 25(3), 22–27. [www.educause.edu/ir/library/pdf/eqm0234.pdf].

5

Sourcing Information Technology Services

Alan McCord

Rising expectations for information technology (IT) services, high deployment and operations costs, and the scarcity of technical and financial resources are leading many higher education institutions to consider outsourcing selected IT services. The challenge of staffing and funding the IT enterprise is driven by a rapidly changing set of dynamics that combine to evolve, and even revolutionize, how campuses operate and how IT leaders conceptualize and implement IT services. In some cases, institutions can effectively and efficiently manage these investments internally. Graves offers an alternative of "relying on virtual operations—that is, contracting or partnering for capital, infrastructure, and services in the Internet economy" (Graves, 2001, p. 48). These partnerships or contractual relationships can be developed not only with private providers but also with other institutions, as well as internally among various campus IT providers. The question is not really one of deciding whether to outsource an IT service but rather of deciding who is best able to provide an IT solution to the campus: in other words, a more generalized sourcing decision.

Regardless of whether an IT investment decision is made in a traditional manner, such as deciding to spend a fixed amount of money over a fixed time to develop a new in-house system using a centralized IT provider, or in a less traditional manner, such as partnering with a set of regional institutions to outsource a suite of services to several private providers, institutions need to develop comprehensive yet flexible decision-making methods that limit neither practical alternatives nor the ability to experiment.

Much of the reticence toward considering nontraditional IT sourcing solutions has evolved from the historic buy-versus-build question, and this question itself likely stems from the historic political and economic isolation of higher education noted in Chapter One of this book. Internal sourcing decisions are often bounded by organizational dynamics, that is, politics.

Today's outsourcing market complicates the situation by focusing on business process services rather than simply the IT services that support those processes. Because IT and business processes are inextricably linked, it is increasingly difficult to make effective sourcing decisions about either area in isolation. This complicates the campus political environment within which sourcing decisions are made.

Forces Affecting Sourcing Decisions

Campuses source their IT services in many ways, some of which are shown in Table 5.1. The most traditional model is to staff and fund an internal IT organization to develop and deliver a broad range of IT services to the campus. This "grow your own" model has its roots in the academic and technical expertise on college campuses that predated the availability of private sector IT services.

The 1970s saw the first commercially packaged administrative systems, which were modified and extended by campuses or by the provider to serve institutions' unique needs. Some institutions sourced the operation of these systems to private service providers, while usually retaining internal control over academic computing operations. As campus computing services evolved to encompass networking and personal computing services during the 1980s, most campuses developed IT capabilities in academic units to deliver

Table 5.1. Types of Sourcing Arrangements

Arrangement	Example
Central provisioning	Delivering IT services from one or more centralized campus IT providers
Decentralized provisioning	Delivering IT services from multiple departmentally centered IT providers
Federating	Coordinating service responsibilities among campus IT providers
Professional consulting	Strategic planning, requirements gathering, and system selection
Contract staffing	Contracted technical resources to supplement in-house staff for fixed-term projects
Project implementation	Project management, technical staffing, and migration and integration services
Services management	Data center operations, help desk operations, repair services, Internet service provider services
Remote hosting	Administrative systems, Web services, e-mail services, course management systems
Application service provider	E-procurement, course management systems, videoconferencing
Microsourcing	Small, focused service arrangements
Rebadged staffing	Transferring institutional IT employees to another campus unit or external provider
Sale-leaseback of assets	Data centers, telephone systems, network infrastructure, cable plant, and mainframes
Insourcing	Taking back previously outsourced IT services

more focused services than those provided by the central computing organization.

In the 1990s, the demand to integrate disparate administrative systems resulted in a tremendous investment in enterprise resource planning (ERP) systems, solving as well as creating problems (Hagel and Brown, 2001). Campus ERP systems are close cousins to their private sector counterparts and thus provide campuses with the option to outsource ERP operations. Other campus IT services—telephony, dial-up services, e-mail, e-commerce, digital video, Web hosting—have also grown in size and scope, enabling private service providers to compete directly with on-campus IT units to provide these services. The application service provider market, fueled by venture capital investments in the late 1990s, represents one possible view of how IT infrastructure services may be provided in the future.

IT Integration

The integration of IT into the overall institutional decision-making process is the most significant force influencing sourcing decisions. As McClure notes in Chapter One, campus IT units no longer control IT on campus; academic leaders have assumed more responsibility as a result of integrating IT into academic programs. Emerging standards and architectures have given campus IT units new reasons to collaborate—or fewer excuses not to collaborate. Multiple-campus collaborative efforts have increased with the advent of both the ERP and open source software movements.

Hawkins and Barone in Chapter Nine cite the movement away from isolated IT decisions; IT leaders must be involved in IT decisions but cannot assume full responsibility, either actively or accidentally, for making the programmatic decisions that drive the institution's use of IT. Institutional IT decision making is also subject to "pendulum swing" forces, including changes in senior leadership, the natural evolution of academic programs on campus, the institutional attention span associated with expensive long-term initiatives, and the impact of government regulations.

Funding Mechanisms

Funding also significantly affects sourcing decisions. In Chapter Four, Smallen and McCredie point out that many institutions still view IT projects as one-time expenditures rather than long-term investments. This view can limit the nature and growth of campus IT infrastructure to the availability of uncommitted funds and can limit the institution's ability to commit to long-term service relationships with on-campus or private providers.

The outsourcing of IT does not generally result in overall cost savings due to service provider "uplift." For example, outsourcers will generally raise ("uplift") staffing costs by approximately 30 percent, not only because of profit margins but costs of recruitment, training, paid time off, and the cost of turnover—costs that campuses generally do not address, especially at the department level.

Campuses can expect that insourcing or federating services may result in additional administrative and coordinating overhead, and perhaps some duplication of services. For any sourcing decision, the cost difference between any current and proposed service arrangement needs to be balanced with anticipated service level or competitive improvements.

Technology and Industry Trends

Technology and industry trends also shape sourcing decisions. The life cycles of IT components, changing demand levels for services, and technology adoption cycles (both planned and accidental) require "awareness of the exponential properties of many variables" (Boettcher, Doyle, and Jensen, 2000, p. 3). The evolution of IT services, from experimental to boutique to commodity status, provides opportunities to re-source services if life-cycle stages can be tracked and managed. Issues of scale also affect sourcing decisions from perspectives of infrastructure, end user support, and availability of alternative providers. Finally, emerging IT industry trends such as Web services, subscription-based software services, remote systems management, and the open source movement can provide new opportunities—or impose new risks and constraints—on the range and quality of sourcing options available to campus leaders.

What Services Should You Consider Outsourcing?

Candidate IT services that could benefit from outsourcing vary widely and are often unique to a particular institution. Some of the variables to consider in evaluating the potential for outsourcing are shown in Table 5.2. In general, services that are provided on an institution-wide scale and are being provided in an efficient and cost-effective manner have the best potential to attract a number of qualified service providers. Many institutions consider outsourcing common infrastructure, such as telephone or network services, and commodity services, such as equipment repair or e-mail provision. Campus decision makers need to be mindful that many of these services are built on significant capital assets, such as the campus cable plant. Consideration of these assets needs to be factored into sourcing decisions. Other services, such as disaster recovery and enterprise security, may be good outsourcing candidates due to their high cost of development.

Poorer candidates for outsourcing include specialized services that are provided to subpopulations of the campus community or are provided in unique ways to multiple communities. These services often lack the scale needed to attract qualified service providers. New and emerging IT services whose adoption cycle is not yet understood are also poor candidates for outsourcing. Service providers need longer-term usage-based commitments to lower their costs, and emerging technologies add risk to their pricing calculus. Many campuses find that these more specialized services are better

Table 5.2. Some Variables Affecting Outsourcing Decisions

Variable	Example
Availability	Current staffing may not support around-the-clock services required for mission-critical services
Elasticity	Relationship of usage level to cost structure
Sunk capital costs	Previous capital investments in physical plant, staff, hardware, and software
Entry cost	Capital and staff training costs associated with starting an IT service
Experience	Advantage of prior experience
Growth and scalability	Ability to respond quickly to usage levels and infrastructure needs
Maturity and standardization	Mature and standardized services are subject to cost reductions by aggregation
Ownership	Institution decisions regarding capital items or sensitive IP assets
Providers	Number of qualified service providers
Security	FERPA, HIPAA, and other regulations

served by internal sourcing to an academic department or service unit rather than outsourcing.

The poorest candidates for outsourcing are IT services that comprise true campus-specific intellectual property. Although these services are rare, they are generally associated with research and development, instruction, and technology transfer.

Institutions may have policies and practices that they view as yielding competitive advantage. The IT services that support those practices would also be poor candidates for outsourcing, because the risks associated with a failed decision are high.

Sourcing IT services does not necessarily mean outsourcing to a private sector provider. Campuses should also consider sourcing options that are available within the institution, including insourcing, collaborating, or federating, as well as among other institutions through collaborations and joint operating agreements. Recently, higher education institutions have begun to collaborate on integrated interinstitutional ERP systems as well as on open source software development initiatives. Examples include the E-Book project of the Committee for Institutional Cooperation (see www.cic. uiuc.edu) and MIT's DSpace effort (see www.dspace.org/).

Many campuses possess several IT providers capable of providing scaled IT services to large segments of the campus community. These units have specialized capabilities that are often linked to faculty researchers and in many cases can deliver focused IT services at higher service levels than by leveraging a central IT service unit. Among the service areas most widely insourced are library catalogue services, administrative systems, scientific computing, and research computing.

In some cases, campus infrastructure services are most effectively delivered by a federated group of IT service providers, each focusing on different primary end user communities but collaborating on technology architecture and infrastructure operations. A good example would be a campus medical center operating its network infrastructure in collaboration with a central IT service provider that manages the rest of the campus network.

If a campus decides to source an IT service to an internal IT provider or federation, a number of actions will maximize the chances for success—for example,

- Establishing cooperative service-level agreements between service providers

- Establishing agreement on common costing, funding, and service-level models

- Establishing common compensation models and a "no raiding" staffing environment

- Ensuring ongoing communication among service providers, colleagues, and customers

- Conducting periodic evaluations of service levels and identifying and resolving service delivery issues

The Sourcing Decision Process

A process for making thoughtful IT sourcing decisions should begin with understanding the potential positive and negative outcomes of those decisions. Real or perceived costs may increase or decrease if the economics of a sourcing decision are at odds with existing campus models. Service levels may change in both planned and unplanned ways. Human resources and cultural issues may arise depending on the match of policy and practice between the institution and service provider. And successful or unsuccessful implementations of sourcing agreements can have political consequences, both positive and negative. These outcomes can result from making any sourcing decision: investment in an on-campus unit, migrating services from one campus IT provider to another, entering into an interinstitutional collaboration, or outsourcing.

Institutions should also identify situations in which IT sourcing decisions will be more difficult to make. Sourcing decisions are tougher when academic and IT decisions have historically not been linked. Decisions will be more complex when the institution is decentralized and has many IT providers. As with most other decisions, sourcing decisions are riskier when made in the midst of a crisis—administrative, operational, financial, or technical. Sourcing decisions are tougher to make when IT services are not already provided efficiently and effectively; this may mean that the campus does not have a good grasp of cost or service provision issues.

Viewing IT Services from a Business Perspective

Quality sourcing decisions cannot be made without the commitment to evaluate and view IT services from a business perspective, especially if outsourcing is being considered. As Hawkins and Barone remind us in Chapter Nine, higher education institutions often reject the business model and resist evaluation. To counter this historic posture, campuses should engage academic leaders, IT providers, and financial administrators in devising rules for making sourcing decisions that are driven by campus values (McCord, 2002).

Economic models should be collaboratively developed, should be defensible, and should be supported by solid metrics and measurement systems. Sourcing decisions are made more difficult when internal economics are not well defined or when multiple funding, cost allocation, and charge-back models are used. (See Chapter Four for a more extensive discussion of IT funding models.) In developing economic models, campuses should understand the differences between expenditures and costs and how to roll up costs into meaningful measures that link to IT services and institutional outcomes (Kaludis and Stine, 2001).

Campuses should develop methods for determining which IT services could benefit most from being sourced to a campus provider, federated, or outsourced. Once potential sourcing providers have been identified, a formal selection process should be used, even if on-campus sourcing is being considered. The selection process allows the institution to clearly identify its expectations and for providers to clearly identify their capabilities and costs. Provider proposals should be carefully analyzed to predict not only their direct costs but also their indirect cost impact on academic and business units. Life-cycle cost assessments are especially important if assets will be sold, leased, acquired, retired early, or abandoned as part of a sourcing agreement.

Even with an understanding of today's requirements in hand, campus leaders will need to develop contingency plans and maintain a flexible future outlook. The higher education and technology environments continue to change rapidly and erratically and, as McCredie (2000) points out, "We will almost certainly misjudge the timing of significant changes" (p. 15). Campus planning and decision-making strategies must be capable of adapting quickly and nimbly as technology and business trends raise new opportunities and obstacles.

Understanding the Negotiating Perspectives

As the campus evaluates proposals and negotiates with outsourcing providers, it is important to understand the negotiating perspectives of both customers and providers and the barriers to understanding these perspectives fully. In deciding to re-source an IT service, the campus generally desires to improve service delivery, control or reduce costs, or take advantage of new technologies. At the same time, the campus wants to establish a manageable relationship that minimizes future risk while providing flexibility to pursue other options as they become available. The campus also generally exhibits considerable concern for the well-being of staff members who are affected by sourcing decisions.

A sourcing provider needs to understand clearly the specific requirements and service level expectations of a client so it can properly staff and manage the relationship. The provider should reduce its risk by gaining a commitment from the campus for a high volume of a standard service over a long time period. The provider should also establish a manageable relationship that will provide it with the opportunity to leverage its relationship with the customer to attract additional customers.

Thus, the customer often desires flexibility with cost controls, while the provider often desires specific requirements and long-term commitments. If these countervailing perspectives are not well understood, conflicts can arise during the selection and negotiation process.

Mitigating Existing Institutional Barriers

An effective decision process must also mitigate existing institutional barriers to making good sourcing decisions—for example,

- Existing internal cost allocation models can skew an institution's perception about the true cost of IT services.

- The campuswide distribution of IT talent can lead to complex and sometimes inefficient service provision models.

- IT organizational and governance structures can place pragmatic political boundaries around decision options.

- Relationships between state and federal governing agencies and labor unions can create decision constraints regarding contracts or personnel matters.

Other potential barriers to good sourcing decisions are shown in Table 5.3. These barriers sometimes become visible when sourcing to an on-campus provider, but are more likely to become visible when outsourcing or entering into a collaborative agreement with another institution. Previously hidden costs can be expected to appear in the form of an explicitly contracted charge, so it is helpful to understand these hidden costs before engaging in negotiation.

In Chapter Two, Penrod notes that institutions' planning styles range from highly formal to highly informal. Although some campuses may be able to execute a successful internal sourcing decision using an informal process, external collaborations or sourcing agreements require considerable rigor in partner selection and contract negotiation to ensure success. Campuses generally use experienced outside consultants and legal counsel for large-scale outsourcing decisions and contract negotiations.

Table 5.3. Examples of Sourcing Barriers

Barrier	Example
Fiscal-year general fund versus multiyear view	Difficult to establish life-cycle costing or commit to long-term contracts
Distributed planning and budget authority	Administrative overhead, diverse support environment, redundancy
Lack of costing and service-level data	Difficulty establishing service requirements or baseline costs
Reservation versus demand-driven model	Difficulty migrating to model where all services are charged for
Lack of fully loaded charge-back experience	Political fallout when the true costs of IT services are recognized
Multiple marginal costing	Campus units may hold different beliefs about IT costs
Human resource issues	Reassigning employees to new employers or having outside employees work on campus
Multiple support platforms	Increased support costs
Historic practices posing as policies	Customized services and higher costs

Improving Your Chances for Success

Once a sourcing decision has been made, the campus needs to provide ongoing support to ensure that the agreement is successfully executed and benefits are realized. This begins with active executive sponsorship and is accompanied by assigning talented administrators to manage the agreement. Particular attention should be paid to the transition plan, because this activity sets expectations for how the agreement will be executed and monitored.

In any sourcing situation, especially an outsourcing agreement, solid disaster recovery and business continuity plans need to be developed as outlined by McMillan and Sitko in Chapter Eight. Managing an outsourced service is sometimes more difficult than managing in-house personnel, so administrators should develop a well-documented management program that includes ongoing service level measurement, problem reporting and resolution procedures, and continuous improvement methods.

Campuses making outsourcing decisions should be prepared to change how they conduct business, especially confronting the thorny issues of simplifying and standardizing processes and services. Long-standing practices often are viewed as policy across the institution, and highly personalized and customized service delivery to specific communities or individuals is commonplace. For example, should the campus maintain a second (or third or fourth) groupware environment? Should the payroll office maintain seven payroll cycles for different employee groups? Should individual academic units maintain separate admissions systems? Should the campus ensure access to institutional IT services from diverse workstation platforms? If a campus chooses to outsource IT services, it will be faced with paying real dollars for each degree of customization and personalization.

Any outsourcing decision should be made with the understanding that the IT service may be brought back in-house or re-sourced to a different provider at the end of the agreement. So in addition to initial transition planning, institutions should prepare a termination and migration plan, remembering that transitions and migrations can magnify known risks. The insourcing process should include clearly defined exit points and associated migration plans, and these plans should be referenced in the contract. Institutions should seriously consider maintaining a retained IT service organization to ensure that the institution understands the re-sourced IT architecture and service model and to serve as an expert group supporting the migration process. The retained IT service organization should develop and periodically review detailed migration and contingency plans in consultation with the sourcing administrator. Sample tasks for inclusion in these re-sourcing scenarios are shown in Exhibit 5.1.

Conclusion

Making IT sourcing decisions entails the same decision-making processes, regardless of whether the campus is considering shifting responsibilities to an on-campus IT provider, collaborating with another institution, or outsourcing to a private provider. Good IT sourcing decisions require deep knowledge of the current business and technology situations, a solid understanding of existing costs and service levels, a clear articulation of future service objectives, and an understanding of the terms and conditions under which future services will be provided.

Exhibit 5.1. Sample Re-Sourcing Tasks

- Administrative and technical migration

- Hardware and software inventory

- Facilities and infrastructure impact

- Restaffing, retraining, and supplemental staffing

- Service migration plan and testing

- Migration and parallel operations planning

- Acceptance testing

- Return of physical assets and backup media

- End user documentation and training

- Legal review of contracts

- Closing accounting and billing processes

IT sourcing options are complex and do not generally fall cleanly into either the "build and run everything yourself" or "always buy from someone else" categories. Every campus should approach sourcing options with the understanding that simplistic solutions will generally not be in its long-term best interest. As Lacity and Willcocks (2001) point out, "Those who approach outsourcing in all-or-nothing terms either incur the great risks involved in total outsourcing, or forgo the potentially considerable benefits of selective sourcing by committing to a policy of total insourcing" (p. 185). Any decision to significantly change the overall direction of IT or the sourcing of IT services represents a moment of truth for campus leaders.

As Penrod points out in Chapter Two, decisions are bounded by the degree of risk that campus leaders are willing to take and should be made with roles and responsibilities clearly defined. Transparent decision-making processes are critical because campuswide sourcing decisions often have an impact on existing institutional practices and economic models; poor decision making can result in lower service levels or services that are merely added to existing programs at additional cost to the campus.

To support IT sourcing decisions, campus IT leaders and their service organizations need to adapt culturally to a world that seems to be becoming less focused on internal technology provision and more on collaboration and partnerships and to avoid the negative interpretations that internal IT organizations often associate with any nontraditional sourcing decision. To move in this direction, IT leaders should evolve their thinking from that of a technical manager to that of a campus process facilitator and IT services architect.

As their institutions consider sourcing decisions, IT managers should ensure that these decisions are not made in isolation, but rather in collaboration with colleagues both within and outside the institution. Most institutions are making somewhat similar decisions about somewhat similar problems within somewhat similar boundary conditions, and thus should make an active effort to learn from one another. As the noted technologist Mark Twain observed, "History may not repeat itself, but it does rhyme a lot."

References

Boettcher, J. V., Doyle, M. W., and Jensen, R. W. *Technology-Driven Planning: Principles to Practice*. Ann Arbor, Mich.: Society for College and University Planning, 2000.

Graves, W. H. "Virtual Operations: Challenges for Traditional Higher Education." *EDUCAUSE Review*, 2001, 36(2), 46-56. [www.educause.edu/ir/library/pdf/erm0123.pdf].

Hagel, J., and Brown, J. S. "Your Next IT Strategy." *Harvard Business Review*, Oct. 2001, pp. 105–113.

Kaludis, G., and Stine, G. "Strategic Management for Information Technology." *EDUCAUSE Review*, 2001, 36(3), 48–56. [www.educause.edu/ir/library/pdf/erm013b.pdf].

Lacity, M. C., and Willcocks, L. P. *Global Information Technology Outsourcing: In Search of Business Advantage*. New York: Wiley, 2001.

McCord, A. "Are You Ready to Discuss IT Outsourcing on Your Campus?" *EDUCAUSE Quarterly*, 2002, 25(1), 12–19. [www.educause.edu/ir/library/pdf/eqm0212.pdf].

McCredie, J. "Planning for IT in Higher Education: It's Not an Oxymoron." *EDUCAUSE Quarterly*, 2000, 23(4), 14–21. [www.educause.edu/ir/library/pdf/eqm0042.pdf].

6

Resolving Information Technology Policy Issues on the Networked Campus

Tracy Mitrano

Policy is important (McClure, 1998). Policies and policy development have assumed an increasingly central role in higher education for three principal reasons: (1) policy (or lack thereof) is often related to legal liability; (2) the complex structure of academic administration requires explicit operating manuals; and (3) multifaceted and complicated relationships continue to emerge between academic institutions and government and the market. Thus, it is now common for most colleges and universities to support a compendium of policies ranging from a campus code of conduct to environmental health and safety regulations to matters of budget and finance, human resources, legal governance, and information technologies.

The larger the institution is, the more likely it is to support a comprehensive library of policies, but it is important to note that no one-size-fits-all policy, or policy development process, exists. Policies and the policy development process should always strive to embody the traditions, culture, and personality of an institution while serving the special mission of higher education overall.

I thank Steve McDonald, whose work has always been an inspiration, for his guidance in shaping and reviewing this chapter.

The Special Role of Information Technology Policy

In an era in which technology has captured the imagination of higher education and become critical to day-to-day campus communications and operations, information technology (IT) policies have assumed a preeminent role in the overall policy development of colleges and universities. All constituencies want and need to know the rules of the road for appropriate use, maximum efficiency, and heightened security of IT resources. But because these resources are relatively new and, depending on one's perspective, either exciting or formidable—or both—in their potential for changing research, teaching, and administration, it is tempting to subsume under the IT policy purview administrative policies or functions that do not properly belong there.

For example, electronic communications can be readily used for assault, but assault does not begin and end with a computer. Images of non-obscene adult pornography on a computer screen, while not illegal or, on most campuses, even a violation of policy, may nonetheless contribute to a hostile workplace in certain circumstances. Likewise, an employee may spend five hours a day glued to Internet pornographic images, or use the university computer and network to run a business, or download voluminous amounts of digital material on her favorite hobby, or file-share copyright-protected materials for which he does not have permission. The list of hypothetical problems goes on, but the lesson is clear: policy advisers for information technologies should take special care not to overextend the bounds of their jurisdiction. The ubiquity of computers and network systems does not mean that every behavior that transpires on them is an IT policy issue. Institutions should avoid creating new IT policies when and where it would be more prudent to focus efforts on applying an existing body of policies to the IT environment.

Thus, in the hypothetical case about the employee who exhibits computer images of pornography on his or her office computer, creating a potentially hostile work environment, it makes more sense to have the human resource department initiate a careful process of progressive investigation into the matter rather than to jump right into the monitoring of electronic communications; otherwise, the institution might run the risk of creating a debate about privacy in the midst of a potentially serious sexual harassment investigation.

Similarly, the excessive use of institutional resources should not be limited to or singularly highlight the electronic medium. Nevertheless, it may be not merely a good idea, but part of a compliance package, to maintain a specific IT policy on resolution of notices on copyright infringement or software piracy. Although intellectual property agreements do not uniquely fall under the purview of IT, developments such as distance learning often initiate discussion, review, and revision of existing policies. Both the insight that central IT administrators bring to those discussions and the investment they have in promoting teaching, learning, and technology projects necessitate that they play a significant role in such discussions. Thus, distinguishing those boundaries is a critical exercise. It keeps IT policies lean and to the point while maintaining mutually beneficial relationships with the associated offices with which policy officers work, such as legal counsel, judicial administrators, human resources, police, and auditors.

This chapter examines the work that needs to be done in the area of IT policy development. For institutions that already have existing policy in this area, guidelines and resources for updating policies are offered.

Policy Development and Management

An appreciation of policy requires an understanding of at least the broad outlines of the policy process. Three models for policy development and management stand out: the centralized policy development office model, the decentralized model, and the hybrid model.

In the centralized model, the highest leaders of the institution—that is, the president or provost—authorize a specific policy office to be the central repository of campus policy and to deploy its personnel in the service of executing a uniform procedure for formulating and issuing policy. Critical to this office is a set of criteria that qualifies a policy for centralized development (such as application of the policy to the institution overall) as a means of distinguishing institution-wide policies from department or local ones. The template for formulating and issuing institutional policies generally includes a policy statement, the reason for the policy, information about to whom (campuses, offices) the policy applies or whom the policy is specifically intended to affect (particular constituencies), and the approximate combination of background information, policy specifics, procedures, responsibilities, and reporting structures. (For an illustration of a policy on formulation and issuance of policies, see www.univco.cornell.edu/policy/pop.for.html.) Creating standing committees with representatives from offices and constituencies around campus that are specifically focused on IT, and even a Web site devoted to policy developments, can assist in the review and communication of policies.

Perhaps not coincidentally, large, decentralized universities seem to gravitate toward this centralized model, probably as a counterbalance to their own decentralized administrative structures. Cornell University and the University of Minnesota are two such examples (see www.univco.cornell.edu/policy/home.html and www.fpd.finop.umn.edu).

Conversely, an institution with a strong central administration, such as Georgetown University, does not appear to require a centralized policy office. Policy development in the decentralized model is instead left to the individual departments or units, with the underlying understanding that should a conflict between them emerge, a robust and authoritative administration will act as the arbiter of the dispute.

Most institutions use a hybrid model in which some aspects of policy development are centralized and others are not. Some colleges and universities may employ a select group of administrators or constituent representatives to vet policy, but may not have formalized either that membership or the process by which the vetting occurs. Other large universities, for example, Kansas and Michigan, do not have a central policy office but do issue university-wide policies under the authority of the president, provost, or key members of the central administration (see www.ku.edu/~vcinfo/IT_policy/index.htm and www.umich.edu/~policies/). The "marbling" of policy in operations and service agreements is yet another variation, one notably deployed by the Massachusetts Institute of Technology.

The ubiquitous role that information technologies play in higher education makes these distinctions among models for policy development significant. From the start, IT professionals, particularly IT policy advisers, must align with the administrative forces that will inevitably have an impact not only on policy principles but also on process, formulation, and promulgation. In addition to working out the calculus of policy development in general, a policy adviser must weigh the application of a particular policy to the central organization or to the entire distributed network. Institutional size, architecture, and culture as separate issues, as well as taken together, are often important additional considerations (Vernon, Mitrano, and Poulsen, 2002).

The First Generation of IT Policy: Acceptable Use

Acceptable (or responsible or appropriate) use policies were among the first kinds of IT policies to emerge in the late 1980s and early 1990s. An acceptable-use policy generally set some basic ground rules for the use of computers and network systems and often included in one comprehensive policy a multitude of issues that today are more likely to be addressed in distinct policies, for example, security ("no sharing of passwords"), privacy ("the university does not monitor electronic communications as a routine practice"), data retention ("the central computing organization shall retain logs for six months"), and responsible use ("no violations of law or policy").

The broad frameworks of such policies served to educate the community and bring together many distinct campus constituencies (Graves, Jenkins, and Parker, 1995). These policies gained considerable recognition on campuses throughout the 1990s and continue to provide a necessary foundation for all other IT policy development.

Around this same time, individuals charged with IT policy coordination started to seek each other out and engage in discussions of related policies and practices. Guidelines and considerations for developing IT policy began to appear in professional publications. In the mid-1990s, Stager, Rezmierski, and Pinkerton (1996) offered a comprehensive overview of the policy environment in colleges and universities, identifying emerging policy challenges related to e-mail, digital signatures, racial electronic terrorism, institutional records in an electronic environment, handling of personal information, and libel. Their work identified a set of enduring principles to help clarify issues as belonging to a continuum of campus values. Hodges and Worona (1996), then codirectors of the Computer Policy and Law (CPL) Program at Cornell University, examined the legal underpinnings for creating campus policy, focusing on five common policy areas: adult material, harassment, privacy, commerce, and copyright.

What accounts for the success of these early efforts to develop IT policy about acceptable use of information resources and technologies in the complicated landscape of higher education?

First, they often emerged in tandem with the creation of centralized campus policy offices or policy development initiatives, regardless of model. Once again, the symbiotic relationship between policy development in general and IT policies in particular is worth noting. As networks crossed colleges and universities, their very functionality presented the question of institution-wide policy in order to maintain the security, manageability, and appropriateness of their use. In turn, colleges and universities began to recognize the need, if not the value, of institution-wide policies to make their rules and regulations uniform, compact, and identifiable.

Second, experience was in many ways the mother of invention. As users of college and university networks explored the legal and logical boundaries of computers and network systems, IT professionals began to identify certain behaviors that benefited the institution when applied uniformly, such as the prohibition of sharing passwords or the use of "netiquette." Then again, there is nothing like a crisis to beget an opportunity. The propagation of a computer worm by an undergraduate student at Cornell University in 1988 resulted in the creation of the oft-cited Abuse of Computers and Network Systems policy (www.cit.cornell.edu/computer/responsible-use/abuse.html) that became the foundation of many acceptable-use policies in American higher education: "Legitimate use of a computer or network system does not extend to whatever an individual is capable of doing with it."

Such experiences informed those responsible for networks of the need for IT ethics education for the entire campus community. Policy, and the policy development process, served the dual purpose of establishing the rules and educating users. Campuses that took the lead in acceptable-use policy development generated resources for other colleges and universities. Cornell's CPL program, for example, created a Web site that housed myriad policy-related materials, most notably the policy compendium, a library of acceptable-use policies from around the country.[1] Of even greater importance, a community of IT professionals emerged who cared about and worked toward the sharing of good ideas, best practices, and communication of new developments.

IT Policy Today

In the past few years, campus IT departments have begun to develop a number of additional IT policies, covering such areas as mass messaging, domain naming, privacy, data access and use, and security. The trend is to develop separate policies in these areas, distinct from the all-encompassing responsible- or acceptable-use policies. In addition, many campuses are looking to update those earlier broad policies in the face of rapidly changing technologies.

Institutional Data Access and Use Policy

Perhaps the broadest category of IT policies apart from those that deal with acceptable use encompasses policies about access to and management and use of institutional data (also referred to as electronic records). Like acceptable-use policies, these policies have a "kitchen sink" quality, bringing everything into the mix, from the library archivist's duties, to complex enterprise resource planning (ERP) applications, to the registrar's databases, to the IT manager's network flow logs. Unlike acceptable-use policies, however, data use policies do not accommodate all of those responsibilities so easily.

At Cornell University, for example, data access and use policies have had mixed success. Currently, an institutional data policy makes simple statements about the responsibility of "stewards" and "custodians" with regard to institutional data, providing a comprehensive policy statement and skeleton outline of responsibilities that, like puzzle pieces, should fit together with more discrete departmental policies. A simple, clear outline of who is in charge of what data transmitted and stored on computers and network systems can go a long way toward resolving questions about access, privacy, and their attendant responsibilities. In the early 1990s, a number of universities successfully established data administration policies (for example, The Pennsylvania State University, Arizona State University, and the University of Michigan). More recently, Indiana University has developed an exemplary set of guidelines for handling electronic institutional and personal information (see www.itpo.iu.edu/InfoGuidelines.html).

IT Security Policy

In these uncertain and dangerous times, there is no more important IT policy development area than security. Axiomatic from the inception of campuswide networks has been the prohibition of sharing passwords, and high-profile incidents such as the computer worm at Cornell produced some of the first statements about security in IT policy. But with the exponential rise in "malware" (electronic worms or viruses) and breach of security incidents in the past few years, not to mention the specter of terrorism since September 11, 2001, security has risen to the top of the list of IT policy concerns.

Just as there is a plurality of campus cultures, so too is there a plurality of opinion on what provisions constitute a solid security policy. Questions about network registries and authentication loom large in this context, and different campuses, according to the architecture and culture of their institutions, resolve those questions in different ways. In this sea of variety, however, IT security professionals, policy advisers, and network engineers seem to be reaching consensus on three courses of action: developing robust security policies, articulating obligations that in different degrees attach to all users of the network, and establishing designated security incidence teams, if not a comprehensive security program.

Developing Security Policies

Not surprisingly, the first recommended action is developing substantive, robust, and enforceable security policies. Given the uneven terrain of policy and policy development across campuses, this recommendation is not as simple as it sounds. It helps to have support at the highest levels of the institution. For example, in the wake of serious security breaches, Indiana University's IT department asked for and received from the board of trustees very strong authority to correct problems with insecure and misconfigured machines on its network that held particularly privileged data. That the board delivered these authorities to the IT shop in the form of a security policy (see www.itpo.iu.edu/ir.html) speaks to the power that policy can exercise when it is in concert with the most powerful offices and processes within an institution. The educative potential of policy, whether it comes from the top down or through a long, drawn-out process of consensus, is also invaluable.

Articulating User Obligations

Obligations that attach to users represent the substantive portion of security policies. Importantly, these obligations begin at the top of the hierarchy, with administrative heads required to do assessments of IT resources inventories and security and appoint individuals within their units to assume responsibility along these lines.

Systems and network administrators constitute a second category of users with specific duties, such as keeping abreast of security developments and deploying the most current patches, virus protection software, and perimeter protections.

Finally, all users are reminded about sharing passwords and also are put on notice that they are responsible for network security. Thus, users should not be surprised when their access is blocked under circumstances of a compromised computer on the network; rather, they should expect to do everything they can to remedy the situation in conjunction with system and network operators.

In addition to articulating the user obligations, the attention to security incidence reporting, which is sometimes included in a comprehensive security policy and sometimes separately maintained, is an important procedure to consider for policy. (For an example of a site that provides specific direction about reporting abuse, see cio.berkeley.edu/policies.html.)

Establishing a Security Team

A dedicated team of IT security professionals, headed by one person whose explicit charge is to direct security operations, coordination, and education efforts around the entire campus, is impera-tive at this point in the evolution of campus networking. (See Chapter Seven for additional discussion on this subject.) The se-curity risks have become too great to manage without personnel dedicated to the task and, implicitly, the institutional support that recognizes the significance of their work.

Naming a director of security with jurisdiction over an entire campus and granting operational control to that person will repre-sent a strong start toward setting up proper security incident report-ing, virus response teams, around-the-clock bandwidth monitoring, operational password policies for servers, and authentication and authorization management.

Mass Electronic Messaging

Mass electronic messaging policies are a subset of general statements in acceptable-use policies about the responsibility that network sys-tem operators have to regulate the system for optimal functionality. These policies identify administrative offices responsible for the permissions for mass messages, with the term *mass* usually meaning one or more of the major constituencies: faculty, staff, students, and alumni. If the institution maintains an emergency messaging pro-gram, then the policy differentiates between the emergency program and the bulk mass messaging program, usually because the emer-gency program will have a different effect on network performance and therefore will require different procedures.

It is increasingly common to have the university relations or col-lege relations office involved in mass messaging policies in addition to the constituent administrative heads, because that office has a facility with official representations for the institution generally, and most certainly has a responsibility when a message is poised for dis-semination to the entire community.

Given that the overall purpose of mass messaging policies is to reduce institutional spam, the bane of all users' existence, they are usually among the least controversial of IT policies when proposed.

Nevertheless, this does not mean that struggles will not occur among administrative heads over the delegation of responsibilities among themselves. The secret in this policy process for IT personnel is to stand by and not get drawn into their contests, letting them work out the details.

Privacy Policy

If IT privacy policies are not among the most controversial, they are at least some of the most complicated. The distinction between public and private colleges and universities begins to explain why, because the relevant laws apply differently to different kinds of institutions. As extensions of the government, public institutions must take account of constitutional protections that private institutions do not have to consider. Employer–employee law as it applies to private entities with respect to electronic communications has widened that already existing public–private gap.

To date, case law recognizes full ownership and control by the employer of computer systems and their content; this body of case law offers no protection to employees. In practice, the law translates into a no-holds-barred policy on employer surveillance, including monitored transmissions, examination of stored data, and even keystroke technologies (McDonald, n.d.). Thus, while the Fourth Amendment, which covers such matters as probable cause and judicial oversight, plays a role in how a state university or college will govern the search of an employee's desk and computer, it offers no guidance to the private college or university. The law to date would appear to condone what many people would regard as arbitrary and capricious actions, such as routine monitoring for content or keystroke surveillance technologies, practices out of step with other traditions in higher education such as free speech, academic freedom, and academic integrity.

Privacy policies, in this light, take on urgency in both public and private institutions but for different reasons. Public institutions should be sure that their policy does not fall below the legal floor, and private ones may want policy to raise the bar, if only to provide at least a modicum of dignity to themselves as employers, as well as to their employees. Just because private colleges own their networks, it does not mean that employees must work in an environment of hypersurveillance and suspicion (Cooper, 1999).

Students exist in a kind of netherworld of law and policy on privacy matters. Clearly protected in terms of whatever can be defined as an educational record under the Family Educational Rights and Privacy Act (FERPA), students nonetheless should also take a strong interest in matters of electronic privacy, if only to track the uses, and potential abuses, of their e-mail. While their mail may or may not fall under the statutory definition of an educational record, depending on its content (and developing case law), it should be more highly protected than an employee's mail by virtue of the difference in status between a student and an employee. This is underscored by the fact that for many students, their residence hall is also their home.

Such a complicated imbroglio of issues and constituencies can surprisingly be resolved with a few simple statements and procedures. If the private institution prefers to shy away from even the mere mention of the term *privacy* for fear of conveying a right it intends no one to have, then it should at least establish practices that offer assurance that it will not monitor without authorization from the highest levels of administration and, therefore, it is assumed, not do so arbitrarily or capriciously. Two such practices stand out: general statements about monitoring for content and the procedures for accessing content.

The first is a statement applying to all users that it is not the practice of the institution to monitor the network for content, except in cases of reasonable suspicion of legal or policy violations. In fact, a concern that the institution either could not or would not live up to that practice has caused a minority of schools to reverse the intent and instead make it clear in policy that access is open and monitoring is the practice (Young, 2002).

The second practice is to set the authority to access material so high in the administration as to obviate concerns about competitor snooping or paranoia about network administrators reading e-mail. Those practices imply the trust that the institution places in the individuals who occupy those offices to consult the proper authorities when necessary (legal counsel, for example, or the dean of faculty) and to exercise proper judgment in all cases (Spinello, 2000).

Still newer directions in privacy statements focus on policies that concern logging and monitoring of network flow data, specifically regulations on next-step activities that resolve Internet protocol addresses into content information (Rezmierski and St. Clair, 2001). Ultimately, it is not grandstanding statements about privacy but discrete practices that give privacy policies their character (McDonald, n.d.; Mitrano, 2002; see also www.educause.edu/ir/library/pdf/pub3102.pdf and www.cit.cornell.edu/oit/policymemos/privacy.html).

Revising Acceptable-Use Policies

As separate policies in such areas as privacy and security are developed, what becomes of the first-generation, all-encompassing acceptable-use policies?

First, these policies can be trimmed down or bulked up depending on the point of departure. For example, if originally replete with a listing of every possible infraction, it might do well to give back to Caesar what is Caesar's. Harassment provisions are one example. Born in the same era as sexual harassment policies, acceptable-use policies often make mention of harassment as a specific kind of violation. So long as a campus has a strong code of conduct that includes harassment, reiteration in an IT policy is probably not necessary or even appropriate.

In an age where networking has not yet seen the light at the end of the security tunnel, it is important to maintain broad statements that can play a role in the computing nightmare that we have yet to imagine. For example, the statement that "legitimate use of a computer does not mean you may do whatever you technically can do with it" is an excellent reminder to users of ethical and policy imperatives that Internet usage or national law has yet to endorse, regardless of whether there is a separate security policy.

Finally, acceptable-use policies set the stage for other IT policies. Policy revision always presents an opportunity for education. Because the use of electronic communications will only increase with time and because it behooves colleges and universities to teach appropriate use of these resources, revisiting these foundational policies should be a permanent star in the constellation of duties for IT policy advisers and their organizations.

Conclusion

As a ubiquitous presence in higher education, IT plays an increasingly preeminent role in higher education policy development as administrators negotiate new technologies within the context of the traditional research, teaching, and service mission.

Recognizing the distinctions between the existing policies that can be brought to bear on information technologies and the areas in which there is a need for new IT-specific policy development is the first priority of any policy analyst. Ensuring that specific policies respect the institution's traditions and personality while still getting the job done is the second. Working flexibly within the politics and policy process of the institution is the third.

The policy will be the rule; thus, there is no substitute for the careful work of understanding an institution's design and politics, culture and traditions in the process of creating a policy. An intelligent, discriminating, and flexible sensibility should underlie all aspects of policy development.

Note

1. The Cornell Computer Policy and Law Program recently partnered with EDUCAUSE to form the EDUCAUSE/Cornell Institute for

Computer Policy and Law. See www.educause.edu/icpl for the policy compendium and information about the annual policy and law conference and ongoing policy officer discussion group.

References

Cooper, J. (ed). *Liberating Cyberspace: Civil Liberties, Human Rights, and the Internet.* London: Pluto Press, 1999.

Graves, W. H., Jenkins, C. G., and Parker, A. S. "Development of an Electronic Information Policy Framework." *CAUSE/EFFECT,* Spring 1995, pp. 15–23. [www.educause.edu/ir/library/pdf/cem9524.pdf].

Hodges, M., and Worona, S. "Legal Underpinnings for Creating Campus Computer Policy." *CAUSE/EFFECT,* Winter 1996, pp. 5–9. [www.educause.edu/ir/library/html/cem9642.html].

McClure, P. A. "Why Policy Matters." *CAUSE/EFFECT,* Fall 1998, pp. 3–6. [www.educause.edu/ir/library/html/cem9831.html].

McDonald, S. J. "Virtual Legality: An Overview of Your Rights and Responsibilities in Cyberspace." N.d. [www.cio.ohio-state.edu/policies/legality.html].

Mitrano, T. "Privacy on Today's Electronic Campus." *Journal of Telecommunications in Higher Education,* 2002, 6(3), 20-22.

Rezmierski, V. E., and St. Clair, N. *Final Report—NSF-Lamp Project: Identifying Where Technology Logging and Monitoring for Increased Security End and Violations of Personal Privacy and Student Records Begin.* Washington, D.C.: American Association of Collegiate Registrars and Admissions Officers, 2001.

Spinello, R. *CyberEthics: Morality and Law in Cyberspace.* Sudbury, Mass.: Jones and Bartlett, 2000.

Stager, S., Rezmierski, V., and Pinkerton, T. "The 1990s Challenge of Insulating the Institution with 1980s Information Technology Policies." In *Realizing the Potential of Information Resources: Information, Technology, and Services. Proceedings of the 1995 Annual CAUSE National Conference.* Boulder, Colo.: CAUSE, 1996. [www.educause.edu/ir/library/pdf/CNC9513.pdf].

Vernon, R. D., Mitrano, T., and Poulsen, M. "Can Cornell Read My E-Mail? Are My Deleted Files GONE Gone? The Facts About Data Access and Retention at Cornell." [www.cit.cornell.edu/oit/Arch-Init/data_access_&_retention.html]. 2002.

Young, J. "Montana Allows Public Colleges to Monitor Computer Use." *Chronicle of Higher Education,* May 29, 2002, p. 21.

7

Meeting the Cybersecurity Challenge

Ronald A. Johnson, Tracy Mitrano, R. David Vernon

In the pervasively networked and ever more information technology–intensive world of higher education, cybersecurity has become a critical factor in protecting the integrity of institutional, student, alumni, research, and clinical data, transactions, and systems against what is now an era of continuous, automated, and increasingly intelligent and virulent cyberattacks. A comprehensive, institution-wide approach to information technology (IT) security, including policy, practice, and infrastructure, is the fundamental mechanism needed to protect campus operations from potentially devastating internal business interruptions, to guard against campus computer systems' being exploited to launch cyberattacks against other sites, and to preserve the privacy of students, alumni, patients, and employees.

Security infrastructure is now also essential for the implementation of powerful and efficient e-business applications, shared digital library and electronic content environments, and the personalized relationship systems that many colleges and universities see as cornerstones of richer, customized relationships with their internal and external communities. These new strategic applications are directly dependent on an institution's abilities to sustain effective security and to consistently deploy middleware campuswide. Often described as the technology superglue needed for the next generation of wide area network–based applications and content, middleware provides services such as authentication (identifying legitimate users and software processes), authorization (determining what authorities or access someone or something should have), directories (repositories of information about people and resources), and integrated security, including important mechanisms that enable systems to decide whether to trust each other.

Meanwhile, campus approaches to IT security, and the closely intertwined privacy issues and questions, are telltales that will reflect, exemplify, and reinforce—or blunt, diverge, and detract from—an institution's core values and ethics and its basic fabric of trust, trustworthiness, and public safety in cyberspace. In its approach to IT security and privacy, each institution will demonstrate by example, to everyone in its electronic family, what its values are regarding conduct in cyberspace and whether it can be a trusted network partner.

Unfortunately, cybersecurity threats are now growing faster than workable solutions, and much institutional practice in this area achieves little more than a false sense of security. At the same time, the implementation of middleware infrastructure across campuses is proving a challenge because of the intrinsic complexities of the software and architectures, as well as its dependence on scarce expertise that is difficult to extend into departments campuswide. Higher education surely does not need any more challenges, but these threats and opportunities are too strategic to defer or ignore.

Threats to Cybersecurity

Administrators and trustees of colleges and universities live under the abiding prospect of waking up to glaring media headlines about any one of a number of potential security breaches on their campuses: forged student records, release of personal financial information on donors, wholesale paralysis of a campus network or of e-mail or Web services, large-scale electronic embezzlement, identity theft, destruction of databases, and even, with regard to the Health Insurance Portability and Accountability Act (HIPAA), litigation with potential criminal liability or stiff fines over unauthorized release of clinical information from, say, the student health center or a health science researcher's desktop computer.

Still another prospective nightmare for an institution is learning that some of its unprotected computer systems have been used, without its knowledge, to launch a major denial-of-service attack. In such an attack, potentially thousands of compromised systems overwhelm and disable selected targets, including those at commercial and government sites. When this occurs, if the institution has not taken reasonable steps to prevent exploitation of its computer systems, it is not only morally responsible but may also be legally liable for damages and threats to the security of the other institutions victimized in the attack. Because of the alarmingly large numbers of unprotected computer systems found on college and university campuses, higher education has been said to pose a threat to national security and the U.S. economy in this regard.[1] This is another compelling reason to acknowledge the importance of protecting computers everywhere on campus, whether they are on faculty desks, in residence halls, in research facilities, or in public labs.

A third threat, much less visible but nevertheless important, is the opportunity cost of not being able to participate in future e-business, e-content, and relationship systems and initiatives due to the lack of the necessary security middleware infrastructure and the trust fabric that these new ways of doing business will be dependent on.

Higher education's security situation is difficult and getting worse. The sheer increase in the number of computers with institutional and other sensitive information and transactions, and the similar increase in the number of people with authorized access to them, greatly amplifies the traditional threats that people will misuse legitimate access and commit the traditional forms of computer crime like embezzlement and grade changing. This would be challenge enough, but it is monumentally overshadowed by the exponential increase in other cyberthreats, such as pervasive automated snooping, hacking, and the propagation of viruses and worms.

How do these newer forms of cyberthreats occur? Cyberspace is now filled with many evolving species of automated probe-and-scan programs that may probe from a distance or nearby for computer server or PC configurations with security holes that have been left open. Such software scans and probes everywhere it can reach (and it now reaches almost everywhere) for even temporary security holes and other configuration weaknesses that can be exploited. If there is a weakness, even momentary, on any system in a network, it can be found and then exploited with no obvious sign of malicious entry or use.

On the average university campus, huge numbers of servers and personal PCs are set up and maintained (or perhaps *not* maintained is a more accurate characterization) with unlocked doors that in essence invite exploitation. Each can, and often does, infect and threaten other systems. Even at small colleges, hundreds of computers in residence halls might well be unprotected.

Where security holes are discovered, malicious software is automatically installed. Sometimes that leads to an immediate attack or vandalism, password or information theft, or data modification or destruction. But often malicious software is left to watch and collect more data, such as passwords and log-on IDs, which perpetrators use to get direct access to business, financial, student record, payroll, patient, trade secret, or alumni systems and transactions. Being able to steal the right password and log-on combinations can yield a gold mine of illicit access if the person with that log-on ID has access to key IT or other systems.

Some malicious software waits in hibernation for a signal to be part of a denial-of-service attack. Such attacks can cripple the targeted site's network or e-mail services or a given set of servers for hours or days, cause the loss of messages and data, and bring campus, hospital, lab, or departmental operations to a standstill.

Even e-mail and simple Web access have become major vectors for the spread of dangerous worms, viruses, Trojan horses, and other malicious software. Every desktop or portable PC or personal digital assistant (PDA), and soon data-capable cell phone, is now a potential incubator of, launch pad for, and target of probing and snooping, cyberattacks, cybercrime, and ultimately cyberterrorism.

These threats come from everywhere on the globe, now apparently including governments and crime syndicates, but experience shows that an alarming number are spread (and too many conceived and launched) from within a campus itself. But even if no attacks or malicious software ever came from within, they cannot be effectively walled out, because a college or university's networks are necessarily somewhat porous to the rest of higher education and to the world outside. And in any case, colleges and universities simply cannot operate in a world in which they block external e-mail traffic and Web access and thus prevent staff and students from using their own computers and PDAs with other networks (from which they can and in many cases will pick up malicious software).

Weakest Links and Collective Vulnerability

A frightening reality for campus and higher education–wide communities, with cultures dedicated to openness and access, is that within them, almost everyone is dependent on everyone else for cybersecurity and privacy. We all are threatened by single points of security weaknesses in our campus neighborhoods.

The one person who fails to lock the door on a server can undermine the thousands who do. One Typhoid Mary has often infected an entire department, campus, or system. For example, if the bad guys can capture or compromise a person's (say, the payroll manager's or departmental chair's) credentials on a poorly managed or open desktop system or server, that may be able to be used as an illicit entry point into a well-protected payroll, academic personnel, financial aid, or other system. The connectedness, collaborations, and shared cyberspaces that are core values and products of higher education are, at the same time, and especially when supercharged by high-speed networks, powerful vectors for spreading malicious software and for magnifying its sweep and effects.

Unfortunately and unsurprisingly, most of the worst cases of university attacks and compromises occur at what is typically the weakest link: departmental, rather than central or enterprise, systems. Given that a campus's weakest links potentially compromise everyone and everything at the institution, what can be done?

Institutions need to have departments, principal investigators, and all individuals whose computers are attached to the network comply with efficacious institution-wide security and privacy policies and procedures and for everyone to administer their systems intelligently and responsibly. That is a tall order with some punishing politics, some serious resource as well as support and training needs, and some very painful trade-offs.

The Common Good: Reinventing Partnerships

In higher education and elsewhere, the paradigm shift from time-shared central host computers to personal computers (and from central mainframes to departmental or group minicomputers and now servers) brought about something of the technology equivalent of the Protestant Reformation. No longer were faculty, staff, and departments largely dependent on the dispensations and expertise (and controls) of computing center gurus for their systems. Instead, individuals could freely choose their own brands of technoreligion and system management philosophy (or not), guided mostly by their own goals, expertise, and localized cost-benefit trade-offs.

In general, this shift to a model of widely distributed (and typically personally controlled) computers, along with mostly departmentally or group-controlled servers, enabled a huge step forward in empowering faculty, staff, clinicians, and students and in boosting the productivity and expertise of the community. In large, complex universities, it also shifted much of the institution's technology resources, and the control of and responsibility for systems management, to departments. This shift to a decentralized model was in part enabled by and dependent on the relatively small amount of expertise that used to be required to deal with a personal computer or small local area network (LAN) in a fairly innocent early era of networking.

But times have changed, and this departmentalized model is breaking down in dealing with security and middleware requirements, as well as other key technology and environmental changes. Today, dealing effectively with and maintaining the required skills for managing PCs, servers, and LANs on high-performance internetworks in the face of continuous security threats requires considerably greater expertise and skills and sheer amounts of time than straightforward PC or LAN management did before. Computer security in a networked environment has become an arcane and complex (but now universally needed) art, practiced in a constantly changing landscape, and typically requiring highly specialized staff who are dedicated to maintaining those areas of expertise.

Few general systems administrators, including those at departmental levels, are able to cope adequately with these responsibilities while keeping up with the changing technologies of their own departmental computer platforms and applications. And even if departments had the money to hire cybersecurity experts, it is unlikely they could be recruited to and retained at departmental-level positions. The challenges and expertise required to sustain competitiveness in the cyberinfrastructure and IT toolkit in any discipline is in itself usually a difficult and arcane job demanding exceptional subject area and technology expertise. Expecting people with such complex and demanding positions also to sustain up-to-date skills on cyberthreats, related security measures, and countermeasures for a multiplicity of computer systems is at best wishful thinking. Making matters worse is the reality that serious cybersecurity is a goal that is not seen as a relatively high priority at departmental levels.

The same is typically true for the software and standards components of the middleware infrastructure required for campuswide (and in some cases interinstitutional) e-business, e-content sharing, e-learning, and customized portal and relationship applications. Here, analogous to the earlier implementation of TCP/IP (Transmission Control Protocol over Internet Protocol) and the Internet protocol suite across campuses (which often had to displace proprietary departmental LANs forcefully), there is a strategic institutional requirement to establish interoperable middleware tools and consistently employed middleware conventions on a campuswide basis.

The development of such middleware will require a comprehensive effort not only on the part of central IT organizations but across campus departments and higher education institutions at large. This effort will take an unprecedented degree of national partnership, and in many cases it will also require institutional leadership courageously insisting on compliance and accountability for the larger institutional good, in an effort that in leading institutions parallels the effort and political capital and will that were required in the early 1990s to deploy Internet protocols and displace departmental and discipline-oriented alternatives. Internet2 and EDUCAUSE are active and effective leaders in coordinating higher education's middleware evolution and in catalyzing deployments that include most leading research universities as participants (see www.nmi-edit.org/ and middleware.internet2.edu/).

What Institutions Can Do

Comprehensive security programs with strong and conspicuous leadership must be integrated into an institution's culture and values, policies and priorities, network architecture, and operational functions. The following sections suggest a number of principles on which to base a comprehensive campuswide approach to IT security.

Understand the Culture and Values of Your Institution

A well-founded strategy for network security begins with an understanding of an institution's culture and values. Although a number of critical practical issues are at stake, the issues of security and privacy are ultimately questions not of technology, procedure, and process but of human and organizational values, ethics, normative behavior, and the needs of the overall community. Following are some typical questions that need to be raised in this area:

- How does your institution feel about the privacy and accuracy of the information it holds about alumni, students, prospects, research subjects, patients, employees, and others?

- What are your institution's views on acceptable use or abuse of university resources, including institutional data, when that use or abuse takes place in cyberspace? What are the citizenship obligations of interacting in cyberspace?

- How much does your institution seek out and value people's perceptions of it as responsible and trustworthy?

- Does the approach to security and privacy reflect core institutional values?

To these questions, one might attach a corollary:

- Do IT policies and practices at your institution reflect those values? If not, how could they be made to do so?

Establish a Locus of Responsibility for IT Security

With the recent surge in security incidents and the likelihood that this represents a long-term trend, campus IT security has become so urgent that strong consideration should be given to the designation of officers or offices to address security and privacy matters from a campus perspective and provide a clear locus of responsibility for dealing with IT security incidents. Designating such an officer or office creates an implicit contract with the campus community; that is, with the services the officer or office provides comes the promise that the campus community will respect the authority of that officer or office. This is crucial, because that authority may entail decisions that have an impact on usage and administration. For example, the decision that a security officer makes with respect to blocking a problem source of traffic might mean disabling an individual's or even a department's or whole building's network connection.

Campuswide understanding and consensus is the best means to make this approach effective. Associated groups and offices such as the regents or trustees, police, judicial administrators, audit, IT policy, campus policy, legal counsel, central IT organization leaders, and departmental IT representatives, not to mention faculty and student advisory boards, should be involved in the process of establishing the mandate for such an office. Stakeholder buy-in and campuswide education about the importance of IT security accrues in the process.

Establish Policy as an Executive Priority

Serious state-of-the-art security and privacy policies that cover the entire institution (not just central units) are an imperative component of an effective security strategy. But having, and broadly and repeatedly communicating, strong executive support is an equally critical ingredient. Some important questions to ask about policy and the policy process at your institution include these:

- Does your institution have such policies? If not, why not?
- Is there a policy development process? If so, is it centralized, decentralized, or hybrid?
- Is there conspicuous executive leadership and sponsorship of policy, or is this left to the chief information officer, auditors, or administrative staff who cannot get this job done alone?

The answers to these questions are important for knowing how to promote security and privacy policies and enforceable rules. If there is a centralized policy office, its vetting and buy-in processes can be used to formulate and promulgate institution-wide security and privacy policies. If there is not a centralized policy office, the creation of security policies can be used as a vehicle to establish either a policy office or its virtual mirror, that is, a group of the most senior executive administrators to initiate the process and sign off after engaging appropriate constituencies to review and critique the policies. (See Chapter Six for a discussion of the complexities of the policy development process.)

Take an Institution-Wide Approach

Institutional security and privacy and the data and information integrity that support them are dependent on the campus's weakest links. Everyone is to a degree dependent on her or his colleagues to in effect lock the doors. And in many institutions, departments hold as much sensitive personal information on people as do central units. Do institutional policies and priorities actively extend to all departments, subdepartments, and individuals, including students and external users? Is there policy in place requiring both central and departmental units to keep known holes in servers and desktops closed?

The goal of the IT security program should be to make every user (individual and department) in the community own and be responsible for IT security. Because of the overwhelming technical scale and basic human nature factors of security risks, a successful program will depend on achieving this goal.

Although it is important for all departments and individuals on campus to accept responsibility for security, it is equally important not to underestimate the need to orchestrate, moderate, and lead such efforts campuswide. Uncoordinated implementation of campus IT security strategies by well-intentioned but insular members of the larger community can create not only a false sense of security but a service cacophony capable of undermining the security sought by the whole. For example, installation of network firewalls may interfere with not just network performance but the integrity and capabilities of the network and university-wide security infrastructure itself. And even seemingly good things like the data encryption of critical university information can become a security nightmare if the university has not implemented a campuswide policy addressing the escrow of encryption keys.

Enforce IT Policies

Security and the implementation of security infrastructure (including middleware) are not likely to be seen by everyone on campus as an essential good that they need to be willing to make sacrifices to ensure. To have any hope of establishing and sustaining a reasonably responsible, durable, and future-oriented cyberenvironment, it is essential to have credible enforcement with real teeth. In the security and privacy realms, that means detection, investigation, and in some cases personnel actions or even criminal charges against not just staff but faculty, clinicians, and students. It can also mean unilaterally disconnecting problem computers and LANs and subnets from the network.

Make Security a Component of Network Architecture

Cybersecurity and privacy exist in the intersection of exceedingly complex technology, policy, and procedural domains that often must accommodate local institutional variations. For an effective approach, an institution needs to have an overall conceptual and technical framework that provides a guiding architecture.

Security can be implemented more or less effectively in many ways in a well-designed IT infrastructure. Some institutions attempt to secure the entire enterprise network through perimeter protection, such as firewalls, but these perimeters are easily breached or circumvented though mechanisms as simple as e-mail attachments, and they do not protect from the considerable internal threats that institutions face. At the same time, they often impart a false sense of security that can be more dangerous than having no security at all.

All servers attached to the network should be made secure through passwords, authentication and authorization, properly configured and patched operating systems, virus software, and so forth. All personal computers should be maintained with appropriate antivirus software and system patches, and, if attached to the network directly, personal firewalls may be necessary for all. In special cases where warranted, the packets traversing the network between truly secure end points could be further secured by encryption, although this is a technique mostly relevant to data under protection of federal legislation, such as educational or health records, and traffic involving passwords and log-on IDs.

Colleges and universities must envision and apply an IT security architecture that encompasses the spectrum of their IT resources. And they must forge that architecture with the assumption that the Internet and virtually all campus networks are now, and will always be, insecure. With the acceptance of the inherently insecure nature of IT and rejection of the simple notion that gating campus communities from the world is the solution, there is a good chance that higher education institutions can effect positive change and protect crucial data, transactions, and other resources.

Educate and Train the Community

Adequate security is dependent on having well-trained and continuously informed security technology specialists, well-trained and informed systems administrators and IT staff, and well-informed computer users who understand the basics (and they easily can!). In addition to dedicated cybersecurity staffs, some institutions set up and actively market broad security and privacy training programs, sometimes including student orientation on security and privacy issues. Effective campus programs similarly have strong incident communication mechanisms that alert system administrators and users campuswide of threats, break-in attempts, and newly detected exposures and related fixes. Furthermore, policies that suggest that all users have some level of responsibility for campus security promote education as well as best practices.

Handle the Basics

Even the best and brightest technologies and middleware assemblages are often easily defeated by the reality that people do not always handle passwords and log-on IDs (and even "challenge-response" smart cards) responsibly. Nearly all relevant security infrastructure is based on simple authentication, that is, doing well at knowing and confirming who the person is who is seeking to use the technology resource. Simple but sometimes fatal breakdowns occur when people share, let their PC remember, or allow others to eavesdrop on password and log-on ID information. Unless there is sustained focus on education and enforcement of fundamentals of password and log-on ID handling and responsibilities, even the most sophisticated security and privacy architectures will be defeated.

Similarly, major progress is possible by establishing mechanisms (including inducements and sanctions) to universally install and maintain virus scanning software, to regularly install security software patches on PCs, and to ensure that known holes and exposures are closed on all servers.

Identify and Protect What Is Important

Well-run institutions have formal procedures for identifying and evaluating the mission-critical nature and sensitivity of systems, applications, and data and for ensuring appropriate controls and disaster recovery mechanisms are in place (see Chapter Eight for a discussion of business continuity). Similar assessment and action are needed from a security and privacy standpoint so that priority can be given to providing extra protections for the most sensitive or critical security and privacy exposures and needs. For example, materials protected by federal and state law, such as student records and soon all medical records, should be accorded high levels of security planning.

Critical information, transactions, and computers must have their own tightly managed and monitored security systems that will protect them in the event other security mechanisms like firewalls fail or are circumvented. This means configuring and managing them to survive attacks. Sometimes critical systems are also gathered in safe-harbor physical and network spaces that have significant extra monitoring, protection, response, and recoverability.

Focus First on Prevention, Then Cure

It is typically a lot less expensive to prevent security breaches than to heal them, and unfortunately more and more security problems are leading to largely incurable consequences. For example, how do you get the trust back from alumni (or get the trust of prospective donors) whose personal financial information has been stolen or inappropriately released and used by others for identity theft? Similarly, under HIPAA, failure to take customary preventive actions may be cause for a finding of negligence, maybe even criminal negligence. Given the public effects of such a finding regarding an institution's handling of student health records, what would it take to make the institution (and the victims) whole? That said, a coordinated incident response process can be crucial to containing damage and learning and communicating lessons learned in what is typically a highly teachable moment.

Be Skeptical of Protecting by Firewalls Alone

Even if one tried to build electronic moats around departments or campuses, intractable problems would occur. Firewalls fail, and there will be innumerable back doors that will be vulnerable if the only protection is a firewall. Because firewalls cannot practically be configured to block all file transfer, e-mail, and Web use, they cannot provide sufficient protection. And in any case, building a moat around the campus does not help deal with the significant threats from within.

Kevin Mitnick, a convicted cybercriminal and break-in artist in cyberspace, says, "It's naive to assume that just installing a firewall is going to protect you from all potential security threats. That creates a false sense of security that is worse than having no security at all" (*eWeek*, 2000). No matter what your institution's view of firewalled perimeters is, it is important to ensure the protection of the end point systems in the event that firewalls are circumvented or an attack or threat comes from within.

Proactively Detect and Probe

Effective institutions perform automated campuswide probes of end systems to detect problem systems and vulnerabilities before the bad guys do. Such probing is an important internal campus tool to discover security exposures and react before they create problems and also to help educate and remind the community of the importance of security and to establish a sense of accountability and shared responsibility.

To be truly effective, these sweeps need to include all systems on campus, including those in departments and research groups and in the possession of individuals. When probes are used and offending systems are discovered, security personnel must have the executive and institutional support and political backing required for them to remove those systems from the campus network.

Identify and Implement Best IT Security Practices

A great deal of excellent work and considerable learning has occurred in the field of cybersecurity based on the collective experience of network operators. Out of that experience comes a wealth of information about best practices, promoted and disseminated by a number of organizations (see security.vt.edu, www.cert.org, www.msnbc.com/news/TECHCRIMES_Front.asp, www.sans.org, www.nipc.gov, and www.educause.edu/security). Exhibit 7.1 lists some effective IT security practices in higher education to consider employing.

Conclusion

Maintaining the necessary level of security in the IT infrastructure of higher education requires a substantial commitment on the part of each college and university to educate its academic communities about the importance of computer and network security, rally the necessary financial and administrative support, promulgate effective policies, and create sophisticated network and security architectures sensitive to both security and service needs. Higher education relies on the security and integrity of data, transactions, and computers. It is not an option to allow the bullies, criminals, and now terrorists on the Internet to win the security wars.

Note

1. President George Bush has directed the development of a national strategy to secure cyberspace to ensure that the United States has a clear road map to protect an essential part of its infrastructure. The EDUCAUSE/Internet2 Computer and Network Security Task Force, established in August 2001, is supporting this effort by

Exhibit 7.1. Effective IT Security Practices

- Employ skilled, dedicated security and middleware staff

- Have a well-conceived security and privacy policy framework and architecture that covers the entire institution

- Proactively scan, probe, report, and follow up

- Quickly and broadly communicate newly discovered exposures, viruses, and incidents

- Aggressively enlist the aid of internal and external auditors

- Enforce IT policies; have accountability and consequences

- Distribute and universally require the use of secure application protocols and desktop virus programs

- Employ two-factor authentication (for example, smartcard plus password) for sensitive or critical systems and functions

- Move critical or sensitive systems to specially configured and closely managed server sanctuaries

- Employ campuswide mechanisms to ensure timely upgrade of desktops to more secure operating system releases

- Apply security patches to browsers and applications

- Use end system (including not just servers but also desktops) firewalls

- Garner the resources needed to support security strategies

- Offer training programs to ensure sufficient basic awareness throughout the institution

- Understand and position trust fabric and culture as the positive values and opportunities they are

- Build out interoperable middleware infrastructure

- Engage users, system managers, and policymakers in keeping systems safe campuswide identifying short-term actions and long-term projects to address systems security problems in higher education. For details, see www.educause.edu/security/.

Reference

eWEEK, Sept. 28, 2000. [www.eWEEK.com].

8

Managing University Business Continuity

Marilyn Ayres McMillan, Toby D. Sitko

Simply introducing the term *business continuity* into the vocabulary of higher education leaders and trustees indicates the incursion of information technology (IT) into university and college life. Automated information systems and the technologies that support them are among the institution's most precious—and most vulnerable—assets. Our institutions have become increasingly dependent on IT in the areas of student life, learning, and administration. How to ensure continuity of higher education when we lose access to key people, facilities, information systems, resources, and services is the essence of business continuity planning.

Many information systems hold irreplaceable intellectual property and data. They depend on formal and informal relationships among people to keep them current, and they rely on miles of complex infrastructure that can be compromised by natural incidents and human error, up to and including full-fledged disasters. Although it can be difficult to quantify the true cost of information systems, they certainly represent major institutional investments.

Our thanks to Margaret F. Plympton of Lehigh University for her insightful, constructive comments on an early draft of this chapter. We are also grateful for the tremendous efforts of all of our New York University colleagues, both before and after the terrorist attacks of September 11, 2001, when we all learned new lessons in business continuity management.

To mitigate the risks of losing access to the systems, we must determine which processes are critical during and immediately following a crisis and how quickly each of those processes must be restored.

Challenges for Managing Information Resources

Creating, managing, and preserving intellectual property and institutional records have been the purview of higher education for centuries, but responsibly managing electronic information resources is a relatively new science and art. Technology costs and the rapid pace of technology change do not easily fit into established budget structures. Policies that govern access to licensed, confidential, or proprietary documents must be revisited in the light of on-line systems. Structures and practices that ensure the continuity of business in the physical world are necessary but insufficient to ensure the same continuity when critical institutional assets are on-line. As a result, institutions must rethink their recovery assumptions.

Institutional business involves complex dependencies that must be managed across the organization. Whereas the chief information officer might be responsible for the integrity and reliability of the campus network, the stewards of the data and information that comprise institutional memory reside in departments across campus. Effective business management involves a broad network of individuals, processes, and systems in both the physical and electronic worlds. Sound approaches to continuity planning serve to protect institutional assets, control exposures and risks, and enable proactive management of service interruptions.

Electronic information systems that drive institutional business proliferate not only in central data centers but also throughout colleges, schools, and departments. To manage their budgets or personnel data, deans and department heads may depend on local shadow systems that provide tailored reports. To create and protect their intellectual property, faculty members may store files without applying the best physical and data security practices. Because these institutional assets are scattered across campus computers, managing and protecting them requires broadly coordinated efforts.

The past decade has seen a rapid convergence of previously discrete technologies that support higher education. Although significant differences still exist between how large administrative systems and smaller systems are built and managed, the bright lines that once separated those technologies have begun to blur. Perhaps most significant, the faculty, students, and staff of institutions are likely to use a spectrum of technologies in their daily work. As a result of this ongoing convergence, some campuses see the need to continually change the organizational structures that support information resources. The drivers for these organizational changes can be rooted as much in institutional culture as in technology.

One manifestation of organizational change is the migration of responsibilities between an institution's central IT unit and IT units located in schools and departments. When technologies are not interdependent, local or departmental support for IT allows departments to tailor the IT environments with specialized software applications and locally managed help services that serve departmental needs. With the emergence of newer systems that rely on centralized authentication and authorization services fed from institutional directories, some responsibilities are swinging back to central IT. Managing the continuity of institutional business in this ever-changing environment requires creative leadership and cross-organizational cooperation.

Risk Awareness

New York University is keenly aware of risk, with its main campus located approximately one and a half miles north of the World Trade Center site. The impact of the September 11, 2001, terrorist attack on the World Trade Center was enormous on every imaginable front.

This event, as well as other major incidents, highlights the need to be aware of how different risks affect the spectrum of student life, instruction, research, administration, physical plant, campus utilities, public safety, and public and government relations. What would result from the partial or complete destruction of key buildings and the records they contain? What if the systems that control fire alarms and security systems in residence halls, classroom buildings, or administrative facilities are compromised? How can an institution manage incidents in ways that minimize risks to future enrollment, alumni support, and overall viability? What if campus facilities and systems are functioning, but no one can access them because of environmental pollutants or unsafe conditions? How does an institution operate in the face of long-term inaccessibility to communication infrastructure? Who has the authority to declare a campus emergency, and where are emergency protocols maintained? Where do officials meet when the usual places are no longer available? How does an institution determine how much risk is acceptable? What will insurance providers require in terms of well-articulated, annually reviewed plans? How involved is campus risk management in business continuity planning? To what degree are community and campus emergency plans linked to campus continuity plans? How can the institution serve its community in responding to community-wide or citywide emergencies?

For business continuity to work, many people must be involved. Trustees will want to ensure that the institution has an executable plan. In large measure, the most successful plans will be those constructed with the full support of the trustees and the campus community. Senior officers and academic leaders ensure that plans are developed, tested, and kept current. Typically, the chief operating officer of each business and academic unit will be responsible for the unit plan. Because they will be part of the plan execution, senior officers must articulate clear lines of authority for situations that disrupt normal operations. A continuity plan should designate who will manage the initial crisis and who will be part of the incident management team.

Emergency Preparedness: Wise Investments, Rational Structures, and Good Practices

Awareness that once unimaginable incidents can disrupt university life has motivated leaders to place renewed emphasis on emergency preparedness. Successful preparedness is, as posters proclaimed for decades, no accident. Everyone affected must be ready to do the right things in the right ways, typically over an extended period of time, as an incident unfolds.

With increasing reliance on IT, not only at institutions but also in the wider world, staying prepared to handle emergencies puts IT in a more intense spotlight than ever before. Even institutions with long and successful histories of responding effectively to emergencies must develop their proved strategies to incorporate emerging uses of technology in daily institutional life and in emergencies, as well as the typically distributed management responsibilities for what may become crucial resources.

The right things to do, highlighted in much management literature, can be itemized in a logical sequence. One step need not be fully completed before another begins. Ensuring the continuity of institutional business refers to a coordinated strategy for managing a recurring cycle:

- Risk assessment
- Continuity planning
- Continuity readiness
- Incident management
- Restoration to the new normal
- Perpetuating the cycle

Risk Assessment

Identifying essential IT systems and services, classifying their criti-
cality, and estimating their viability in an outage is the foundation.
The IT systems and services to consider are the ones the institution
runs centrally, the ones run by other offices at the institution for
themselves and sometimes for others, and services acquired from
outside providers. With the evolving reliance on IT for new functions, such as instructional technologies, and in new places, such as
managing building heating, ventilation, and air conditioning systems and access control systems over the network, more resources
than ever before must be considered and more participants than
ever before must be included in the practice.

Three eventualities are useful to consider in estimating how long
an outage an institution can sustain:

- What if the system or service—telephones, networks,
  Web site, e-mail, application, local or central computer—goes down, but people can stay in or get to
  offices, residences, or facilities?

- What if the system or service is running, but people
  cannot stay in or get to sites?

- What if sites, systems, and services are unavailable?

Incorporate time in your thinking. Consider peak and other critical times for a system or service, prime-time needs and off-hours
expectations, and requirements of the academic calendar and business cycles.

A classification scheme helps communicate priorities. Some systems and services fall readily into the category "must have available
around the clock, all year, especially during an emergency." Others
naturally have a much lower priority: "Get back and running whenever things get back to normal, up to thirty days or more after the

outage." Establishing the midrange categories can be problematic because it may be difficult to reach agreement about the priority for some systems and services. Requiring a documented business continuity plan for every highest-priority system and service, as well as periodic participation in continuity readiness activities, can influence the classification decision.

A straightforward risk assessment template facilitates the assessment for each resource and enables aggregation of the information across the spectrum of services and participants. Typically, universities are experienced at such practices for administrative applications. Now may be the time not only to refresh your thinking about those systems, but also to extend your assessment to include the outage risks associated with IT resources supporting all the other elements of university life.

Continuity Planning

Opportunities to improve and perhaps overhaul business continuity management plans will surface in virtually any risk assessment activity, whether it is an institution-wide or department-based activity. Continuity planning activities focus on determining four separate but related courses of action:

- How to conduct business in the event of an outage of systems and services

- What steps to take to prolong the availability of key systems and services in an outage

- What information and training to provide managers, staff, and vendors who will be involved

- What awareness activities and other preparations to provide for the university community

Models developed for managing continuity in the corporate world can be useful, but are only part of the story for universities, especially for those with students in residence, numerous facilities, or substantial public constituencies. It can be useful instead to consider models used by municipalities.

Continuity planning is by its nature iterative and collaborative. Continuity plans for central services influence departmental planning. Continuity needs of departments may drive changes in central service plans. Opportunities to leverage resources are possible. So are possibilities for gaps and misunderstandings. The most inhibiting factor is that continuity planning is usually everyone's fourth priority, on plates already too full. Although it is essential to focus planning activities on the highest-priority elements, it is important and appropriate to encourage broad-based individual and department efforts to get better prepared.

Planning forces an institution to reach a balance between acceptable risk and acceptable one-time and recurring costs. Business continuity planning includes the following steps:

- Building awareness

- Analyzing business functions to assess operational, academic, fiscal, legal, or regulatory risks

- Determining the recovery time frame for each business function

- Identifying recovery alternatives within specified recovery time frames

- Creating, testing, revising, and updating plans

- Revising job descriptions to include continuity planning

Continuity Readiness

Readiness involves executing the elements of continuity plans that prepare people to respond to a disruption. Some elements of readiness must become routine components of everyday activities for many people: refreshing emergency contact lists, running backups, and refreshing batteries in safety kits, to name a few. Some readiness efforts are periodic, such as verifying the recoverability of backups and running a training session for new staff. Others may be one-time large- or small-scale projects for particular units. Central IT staff might add alternate electric power sources for a computing facility. A student services office might relocate or digitize its collection of paper. An associate dean may work with faculty and instructional staff to establish phone trees.

Still other readiness activities entail broader coordination to exercise key elements of the continuity plan. It is not enough, for example, to have alternate sites for system and service operations or for coordination of university emergency management activities. Managers and staff must ensure that the systems and services can be made operational in the sites and readily used at designated locations.

The important tenet here is that continuity readiness is an ongoing responsibility of every senior officer and direct reports and many staff. The time needed to pay attention to this critical function must be factored into individual and group work plans. The ability to pinch-hit in an emergency must be in everyone's skill set. Willingness to collaborate on readiness activities across institutional borders must become an integral component of university citizenship. Capacity to promote this attention, skill, and willingness is a critical success factor for the chief information officer and the chief executive.

Incident Management

Incidents come in all sizes and at any time of day and night. Most institutions have well-exercised procedures for handling emergencies of contained scope and scale. As those procedures have come to rely on IT resources, both local and central, it is important to incorporate their viability as part of risk assessment, continuity planning, and continuity readiness efforts.

Transition of an incident from contained or transient to broad and enduring may or may not be obvious to beholders. It is highly desirable to have developed, as part of continuity planning, a protocol for handling this transition: who will declare the extent of emergency response required; who will be notified; and where, if needed, emergency response centers will be located. Determining centers and participants as part of the continuity plan and maintaining components as part of readiness activities enables everyone to avoid ineffective scrambling when the time comes to mobilize.

In managing our institutions in normal times, we follow protocols of deliberative consultation, as well as various combinations of orchestrated and individual or unit actions. Depending on the nature of the emergency, a similar approach applies to incident management, but with some key differences:

- Time frames for decision making are accelerated.

- The pattern of which actions are orchestrated and which are unit or individual may change.

- Public relations about the institution's handling of the situation may be heightened in all media.

- New developments may or may not radically alter the situation at any time.

This suggests adopting an "accordion" approach in the emergency response center: personnel come together regularly for coordination and then disperse for action in departmental units or as cross-functional teams. Select with care those who need to be in the centers, and conduct departmental gatherings and activities elsewhere. Designate methods and times to reconvene and maintain contact.

At New York University, the primary emergency response center is operated by Protection Services, under the leadership of the chief of campus security. Telephone, radio, network, and computer services at the center are supported by Information Technology Services (ITS). The center includes small offices for representatives of units active around the clock in handling the response, such as ITS, Buildings Maintenance and Operations, Student Housing, and Public Relations, as well as a larger meeting room. In non-emergency times, the center serves a completely different purpose. When warranted, at another location, NYU transforms the ITS Client Services Center and Telephone Switchboard into an emergency call center, staffed around the clock and augmented with volunteers, to assist students, faculty, and staff affected by an emergency.

The work of the chief information officer in the management of the large-scale incident is complex:

- Collaborate with other senior officers to manage the overall response

- Guide IT management in running the IT continuity activities

- Lead others in whatever other systems, services, and problem-solving activities may be required

- Reserve some personal and organizational capacity for addressing the next surprise

- Attend to the human impact of the crisis on oneself, managers, staff, and colleagues

In addition to their planned efforts to support the emergency response center and keep systems and services running, IT staff may be called on to perform any number of previously unplanned activities during the emergency. Some examples include producing data in various configurations, coordinating call center volunteers from many offices, equipping new venues for relocated activities, and acquiring and distributing inventories of special gear. In a broad-based emergency, those staff may also be experiencing personal impacts from the situation, such as problematic transportation to and from work or worries about the safety of loved ones. Consider ways to acknowledge and ease the toll on them, while respecting their privacy.

Restoration to the New Normal

Although the demarcation between the end of an emergency situation and the start of routine operations is often not clearly delineated, it is important to declare the end at a time of the leadership's choosing. Close the emergency response center. Return call center availability to normal hours. Reduce the frequency of emergency coordination meetings. Get some sleep. Appreciate and recognize the participants.

Do not expect things to get back to familiar normal patterns anytime soon. If nothing else, everyone's conception of what is normal now includes a new eventuality that actually occurred, along with everything they learned in that experience. Even more important, leaders, managers, and staff may be exhausted and need time to recover, a rhythm that will vary for each individual. Nevertheless, demands of everyday activities will manifest themselves, with expectations for familiar service levels and response times. Those demands may indeed be heightened in the aftermath. If the institution is concerned about whether current enrollments, future applications, or donor and sponsor support will be adversely affected by news of the emergency, you may choose to work particularly hard immediately to avoid downturns. Such initiatives may well engage many of the service providers now in recovery. At the same time, the various units, IT among them, must assess the impact of the recent experience in the following two dimensions and revise their work plans accordingly.

- What delay, if any, did the emergency inflict on targets for projects in progress?

- What lessons learned from the emergency can be factored into those projects and life in general?

Anticipate that the interest in and tolerance for risk assessment and continuity planning will fall amazingly rapidly on everyone's agendas, even those of the zealots. Make every effort to capture expeditiously the reflections on lessons learned and turn them into visible improvements for the next time—because there will be one.

Perpetuating the Cycle

Changing conditions at the institution, among continuity service providers, and in the wider world dictate that institutions undertake regular efforts to keep their business continuity management plans vital. This can be accomplished at several levels; for example, institutions can

- Publicize reminders of existing plans for the general community at least once during each academic cycle

- Schedule continuity preparedness drills at least once a year

- Establish a process to incorporate new systems, services, and functions in the university plan

- Revisit and refresh departmental and university continuity plans at least annually

- Encourage participation in professional seminars on risk assessment and business continuity

- Develop a regular practice to formally review the risk assessment and plans with senior officers

Chief information officers can be catalysts in promoting continued attention to business continuity, both within the IT functions and throughout the university. Chief executives and other senior officers set the tone that business continuity is not simply the job of technologists; it is a university-wide priority.

The Right Level of Investment

A salient responsibility for senior officers and trustees is determining the right level of capital and operating investment in business continuity management. Arriving at the right answer for an institution can be complicated. Even the Federal Emergency Management Authority, with cadres of experts engaged, is struggling to modernize its cost-benefit calculation models to assess return on investments in disaster prevention projects proposed by nonprofit organizations for funding, as part of its emergency mitigation program. Some rules of thumb may be helpful:

- Risk management is the starting point. What is at risk at your institution in the event of a substantial IT outage? What is your institution's general approach with regard to investing in risk avoidance?
- Prior and current spending levels for business continuity management are a second consideration. Are you getting full value for your dollar, given your latest risk assessment? Can you leverage better coverage from current levels?
- Balancing your IT investment portfolio is another element of the decision of how much to spend in both dollars and staff effort. Although business continuity management is necessary, it likely is not the only IT investment sufficient to meet your strategic institutional needs. A new Web site that might be down for a few hours someday may be preferable to deferring all Web presence until off-site backups are arranged for existing systems—or maybe not. Prioritize and pace investments effectively among your IT needs.
- Building business continuity management costs into the project and operating costs of prospective new systems and services is ultimately the way to perpetuate the cycle. Evaluating the cost-effectiveness of proposed new initiatives should incorporate the incremental costs of business continuity measures—appropriate to the identified continuity classification—in calculating the total cost

of acquisition and ownership. Publishing a template of business continuity considerations for project proposals can be useful.

Conclusion

The right way to do these business continuity activities boils down to the people in the IT organization and, for that matter, throughout the institution and their readiness to be service-oriented and innovative team builders, problem solvers, communicators, and results producers and to be resilient under pressure.

Everything you do to make the IT organization more effective in today's environment positions managers and staff in IT, and throughout the university, to be more effective at business continuity management. Applying ideas articulated throughout this book can make the difference.

Successful business continuity management is crucial. It enables people and institutions to be as prepared as they can be to respond to unexpected disruptions. In serious circumstances, it may protect the health and safety of members of the university community. In extreme cases, it can enable the institution to remain viable, retain students and attract prospects, and sustain the confidence of sponsors and donors for the future. This keeps business continuity management high on the list of concerns of university leaders and trustees. Addressing their concerns requires that the chief executive and the chief information officer exercise the familiar leadership virtues of vision, encouragement, and persistence in this domain.

9

Assessing Information Technology
Changing the Conceptual Framework

Brian L. Hawkins, Carole A. Barone

Higher education is encountering unprecedented pressure for accountability from both internal and external constituencies. Frank Rhodes, former president of Cornell University, states: "Accountability . . . is the newest buzzword for all institutions. It is an important—indeed, a vital—obligation, but it means very different things to different people" (2001, p. 242). These constituencies include trustees, the faculty, the administration, the students, prospective student families, and alumni, each of whom wants something quite different from the institution. The causes are myriad, but internally there are especially strong pressures for the leaders of information technology (IT) units to explain and justify the costs and benefits of the expenses associated with their areas.

This attention to IT is attributable, in part, to the fact that IT is a growing, relatively new, and rather substantial portion of an institution's budget. While this book, quite appropriately, deals with information resources (IR) in the broadest sense, this chapter focuses on IT assessment and the challenges associated with this facet alone, because the nature of assessment in libraries, media services, and other dimensions of IR is too varied and broad to be adequately addressed in the limited space available. This chapter reviews past and current means of assessing IT on campus, discusses the limitations associated with these, and suggests directions to meet the needs of campus leaders in addressing the demands of accountability in a more encompassing and holistic manner.

The chapter concludes with the recommendation that institutional leaders embrace a new conceptual framework to assess the next steps required to sustain progress toward articulated goals. Called *transformative assessment*, such a framework integrates IT within the institutional strategic plan and aligns planning and assessment at all levels with a focus on outcomes.

Shortcomings of Current Models

Historically, three distinct methods have been used in evaluating and assessing IT: satisfaction surveys, various input measures, and self-assessment. Each method has some serious shortcomings, and although they may be useful in specific contexts, they fail to provide the holistic approach to assessment and accountability that is being called for on campuses today.

Satisfaction Surveys

Perhaps the oldest method of assessment is having the IT environment evaluated by the users on a campus through satisfaction surveys. This process has a history that dates back to the mainframe era of campus computing and the desire of IT officers to understand the extent to which the users of their services were being supported. This has been, and should continue to be, a vital part of an overall assessment strategy on campuses, but it has some inherent weaknesses. First, satisfaction data need to be understood in context, because during the past two decades, the user population of campus IT resources has changed from a relatively small, fairly homogeneous, and sophisticated group of users to virtually every faculty member, staff member, and student.

Because IT is still viewed by some within the academic community as causing undesirable change, measures of satisfaction with technology-related services could, in fact, be reporting levels of dissatisfaction with long-held assumptions being challenged. It is also highly unlikely that any campus IT organization can really satisfy all constituencies. The campus IT organization is all too often driven by the loudest and most vitriolic voices on campus, not necessarily the most important or rational ones. IT units are seldom given guidance (not to mention protected or defended) by the administration, because most campuses have an ethos and expectation that all needs should and must be met.

Satisfaction may make life easier for everyone in an emotional sense, but it is not necessarily an indicator of the strategic importance of the role IT plays in accomplishing an institution's core mission. IT investment in infrastructure and services is not and should not be a function of popularity. Satisfaction surveys can be useful in allowing internal success (as perceived by users) to be evaluated (as perceived by users), and this can be very important, but such instruments do not assess the strategic importance or value of an investment. IT is an institutional issue. Setting and managing campus expectations with regard to IT is perhaps the greatest challenge facing higher education leaders. Efforts of the chief information officer (CIO) to do so are often looked on as self-serving and bring into question her or his role and credibility. Thus, it is essential that other senior officers, and especially the president, become involved in clarifying the role of technology in terms of the institutional mission. This cannot be relegated to the CIO alone, because the institutional imprimatur can be granted only by the CEO and other academic leaders.

Input Measures

Like most of the rest of higher education, IT has a history of employing various input measures as indicators of quality, with the implicit assumption that more is better. In other dimensions of the higher education enterprise, the lower the teaching load of faculty, the smaller the student-faculty ratios, the more titles held in the library, and the more students rejected in the campus admission process, the better the institution. With IT, it was such measures as percentage of the education and general (E&G) budget and the breadth, depth, power, and diversity of hardware and software at an institution that served as benchmarks and indicators of quality. All of these are measures of input, with the potentially fallacious assumption that more input (and, implicitly, greater expense) yielded a better product. These measures did not provide indicators of output and were certainly not indicators of efficiency, but more likely were the opposite of that.

For years, the gold standard for IT was captured in the longitudinal survey work conducted at the University of Texas at Austin by Warlick (various dates). These data provided important comparisons among campuses and often served as an effective means to justify investing more heavily in campus IT infrastructure. Percentage of E&G devoted to IT was one of the measures reported in Warlick's survey. This value usually ran between 3 and 5 percent of the core academic budget, and it was seen to rise substantially with the advent of campus networks, microcomputers, and the expansion of IT to all disciplines in the academy. This ratio has now become obsolete because of the declining emphasis on fund accounting as a means of presenting campus budgets. With the technology becoming more fully integrated into the overall fabric of the institution, it is also increasingly difficult to isolate expenditures that are solely for IT (although Smallen and Leach, 2002, have conducted some very useful studies of IT expenditures among predominantly smaller colleges; see www.costsproject.org).

Warlick's research and other similar surveys, such as the CAUSE Institutional Database (ID) survey, conducted annually from 1970 through 1996, and the Campus Computing Survey (Green, 2001) provided much valuable comparative data. Indeed, the new EDUCAUSE Core Data Service launched in the winter of 2002–2003 (see www.educause.edu/coredata) is an attempt to provide leadership with needed understanding of IT functions, organization configurations, sources of IT revenue, and expenditures, practices, and technologies. However, none of these efforts is, or was intended to be, an assessment tool. These measurements of IT investments were often an institutional version of keeping up with the Joneses, driven by the highly competitive marketplace of higher education. Competition for students, various ranking surveys in popular magazines, and research support comparisons, for example, often motivated others within the college or university, besides the CIO, to turn to these surveys.

Although such efforts may have leveraged additional funds (appropriately or not), they do not include measures that offer insight into how technology is enabling new and better research, whether or how technology is enhancing teaching and learning, or whether administrative functions are easier for students to access or less expensive to operate. The problem is that in order to effectively measure the success or value of an IT investment, we must come to grips with evaluating these functional outcomes of the college or university. However, we have thus far successfully avoided grappling with these difficult challenges of assessing learning outcomes, administrative efficiency, effectiveness, and so on. Without working in tandem with others on campus to identify and evaluate these outcomes and then to understand and describe the enabling role of IT in facilitating these accomplishments (or the failure thereof), we will never be able to assess the return on IT investment reasonably and meaningfully.

Self-Assessment

Until recently, the closest that higher education has ever come to any form of assessment that attempts to look at the impact of these investments and the associated outcomes has come under the rubric of self-assessment. In the mid-1990s, CAUSE, Educom, and the Association of Research Libraries collaborated to publish a set of self-assessment guidelines to assist campuses in asking the important, albeit difficult, questions about the impact of IT on campus (HEIRAlliance, 1995). Although some of the questions implicitly approached the subject of outcomes and the role of IT in achieving those outcomes, most of the questions asked about the adequacy of hardware and software availability, governance structures, training opportunities, and so on.

A major shortcoming of the guidelines was that virtually no one in a leadership position on higher education campuses at the time was sufficiently knowledgeable about IT to judge what was adequate for a given campus. These guidelines, however, were very important in providing any kind of standardized and structured means of assessing what IT resources were available and how well they were supported on campuses. Not only did many campuses embrace this set of guidelines, they were incorporated and adapted into the criteria of a number of the regional accreditation agencies, thus playing a very real role in institutional assessment at that time, and in some cases until the present.

IT Assessment in Industry and Higher Education

The history of IT investment in the commercial world is longer than that in the academic world; hence, IT has a more defined set of goals, articulated strategies, and a historic means of measurement in the commercial area. When IT investments are proposed, in industry—and increasingly in higher education—the questions that are asked by senior management have to do with issues such as these: What will be the return on investment? What value will accrue as a function of this investment? Can a cost-benefit ratio on this investment be projected or determined? These financial measures are challenging in the corporate setting and virtually impossible to deal with in the academic setting, because it approaches academic heresy to suggest that higher education is a business or to use the nomenclature associated with a business model. However, as trustees, legislators, and others with responsibility for higher education push for accountability, it will be in the language of business that they will expect responses, unless we have the rubrics at hand to redirect inquiry to more appropriate measures.

Business measures fill a void. Imposition of the quantitative measures of business to determine the outcomes of investments in technology is simply a reflection of the failure of higher education leadership to assume appropriate responsibility for its role in decisions regarding overall institutional assessment. This denial of responsibility is deeply embedded and penetrates broadly throughout academia. Even midlevel administrators, who are closer to the day-to-day decisions regarding the role of technology in their units, tend to deflect assessment of functionality of technology-enabled processes to the CIO.

Yet responsibility for matching the enabling power of the technology to administrative processes and to assessing its fit with institutional custom legitimately belongs with the functional area head. Ideally, such implementations and assessment efforts would be conducted in cooperation with the CIO, but the point here is that ultimately, this responsibility lies with the functional unit head. Higher education needs to craft better arguments and collect data in a manner that can preserve the integrity of higher education and still be responsive and accountable. To attain these goals, it is imperative that other members of senior management be involved and take responsibility for their own IT environments, in conjunction with the CIO.

Assessing Outcomes of Applications Versus Infrastructure

When campuses decide that certain technology investments are necessary to remain competitive in a market (even though the costs associated with these decisions are anything but insignificant and are recurring because of the need for ongoing upgrade and replacement), then these investments should be assessed not as a function of their direct savings, but on their ability to allow other institutional goals to be attained. This is the kind of discussion that increasingly should be held at the time such investments are considered, not after the fact in the face of budget increases for IT that are greater than those of other units on the campus.

One of the most useful conclusions that has been generated from the industrial and commercial world is that a fundamental difference exists between how assessment of IT applications and IT infrastructure should be approached. The Gartner Group suggests that in the area of applications, the criteria for investment should focus directly on outcomes, such as return on investment (ROI) and cost savings, with the value of the IT investment measured directly against the outcomes affected in that application (Harris, Grey, and Rozwell, 2001). In higher education, this would manifest itself in such areas as a new admission system, with the measurement being in terms of number of new applicants, increased yield, or a change in trend lines associated with such output measures.

These outcomes would need to have some dollar value assigned to them to get a true ROI measurement, but with a specific application, such measurement is possible. Similarly, in the implementation of a new development system, better tracking, higher alumni giving rates, and other measures could be translated into direct ROI measures (Knox, 2002). All of these "savings," however, require a plan to capture the necessary data to document and substantiate these findings—something that all too often is missing from a campus implementation plan for an IT application.

The use of such financial outcome measures may be possible with applications but becomes nearly impossible with infrastructure investments. Infrastructure, such as the campus backbone, the level and speed of connectivity of the network, or even public access clusters, creates a campus environment in which it is difficult, if not impossible, to directly identify any kind of definitive ROI or cost-benefit ratio, and the same is true in industry. According to Knox (2002, p. 6), "Unlike IT applications, which are typically linked to a specific business goal, the value of infrastructure is realized over a long period of time through the support of multiple business goals, many of which may not be known at the time of initial infrastructure development. The value of infrastructure is realized through the applications and initiatives it is used to support. Infrastructure in isolation is valueless, just as the foundation of a house provides no value unless, or until, a house sits on top of it."

This approach to infrastructure requires that all divisions and functional areas see the advantage and the need to invest in infrastructure, so that they can achieve their own subunit goals. However, the ability to see this greater good and to make tough decisions that result in a higher "taxation rate" for these services is difficult, especially in times of limited resources and a difficult economy. IT organizations have tended to perpetuate this situation by crafting infrastructure procurement rationales in terms of inputs, that is, power, capacity, speed, and so on.

The University of California System serves as an example of a higher education institution that is beginning to understand the important distinction of looking at IT as a critical investment to achieve other goals, and not as a cost center. The underlying assumptions associated with the new business architecture efforts being undertaken in the University of California System, as they lay out a plan for how they will do business in the future, clearly identify technology as an enabling function, not an end in and of itself (New Business Architecture Planning Group, 2001).

The Gartner Group has recently proposed a useful approach that looks at the value of investment (VOI), a broader and more inclusive concept than just a financial ROI metric. This concept of VOI emerged as a function of the "knowledge economy"; it focuses on leveraging intangible assets and reflects the multiple dimensions of benefits accrued instead of limiting assessment solely to ROI considerations (Harris, Grey, and Rozwell, 2001). This concept is not only more inclusive, it is also more acceptable and compatible with the academic culture, whereas, as previously noted, ROI is certainly not politically correct. The Gartner Group's research suggests that the value of an investment is accomplished through initiatives that increase organizational competencies; enable collaboration among people, systems, and enterprises; implement new leadership methods and capabilities; multiply the impact of networks, whether social (people) or technical (applications or other system connections); and formalize knowledge management and the management of intellectual assets. Learning outcomes assessment is also on the rise. Given the growing significance of the enabling role of technology in teaching, leaders need to pay attention to this dimension of the assessment of the value of investment in technology.

These are all critical outcomes in any organization and are especially important to higher education. They suggest that "over time, this value is increasingly the source of competitiveness, including increased value of brand, new and deeper core competencies, innovation, knowledge creation, increased depth and range of talent, and improved strength and diversity of human and technology networks. Although enterprises intuitively recognize the value in these initiatives, most lack a formal process for assessing expected value and managing the initiative to achieve it" (Harris, Grey, and Rozwell, 2001, p. 5). This is the challenge that higher education faces as we begin to deliberate how outcomes are to be defined and measured within the academy.

In their strategic plans, higher education institutions generally articulate a vision describing the outcomes of their efforts. Assessing the value of investment is a tactical method of focusing on desired outcomes that will lead to the fulfillment of that vision. Transformative assessment is a higher-level strategy for keeping the disparate internal objectives on the trajectory toward that institutional vision.

Transformative Assessment

The term *transformative assessment* is used to describe assessment that is directly linked to the goals of the institution and occurs when the institution's academic and administrative leaderships are genuinely committed to transformative change. The institution is ready to move from asking, "Did we do what we said we would do?" to asking, "What has to happen to move to the next stage?"

According to the READY tool developed by EDUCAUSE, "Transformative assessment occurs when a number of studies at different levels align with each other, and with the process of planning and implementation, so that over time they all help guide and accelerate the desired improvements."[1] Instead of saying, "We have installed Internet2-level networking infrastructure," we need to be able to say, for example, "The installation of Internet2-level networking infrastructure has enabled 225 faculty in the following disciplines . . . to adapt the pedagogy in their courses in the following ways . . . to engage their students in solving complex, new problems in higher level courses." This type of assessment moves beyond simplistic measures—for example, benchmarks of an institution's installed base of technology—to a far more complex and sophisticated assessment of multidimensional progress toward desired goals. The purpose of assessment shifts from what is to the determination of what ought to be. This approach links the planning and assessment processes much more closely. The process involves the identification of a set of desired institutional outcomes together with their manifestation at multiple levels throughout the institution, and the establishment at the outset of the assessment activities that will gauge progress toward their attainment while at the same time surfacing new goals to be pursued along the road to transformation.

Higher education institutions are just beginning to understand the importance of integrating a broad institutional assessment framework, which must include a technological assessment component, within their strategic plans. With the acknowledgment that

IT infrastructure is no longer solely an IT issue, members of the institution's leadership cadre assume mutual responsibility for getting their homework done. For any significant IT investment to be made, senior IT and institutional management must validate that decision; top management must assess, agree, and decree that the investment is worthwhile to the institution. Moreover, they must agree, at the outset, on how the value of the investment in infrastructure will be measured.

The right questions become evident once leadership recognizes its collective responsibility to assess both the existence of appropriate technology and the appropriate use of that technology. Assessment must occur within a collaboratively developed framework, designed to answer questions about the value added by the institution's investment in technology at the time the investment is being planned.

Transformative assessment is a collaborative activity because it must measure change in multiple dimensions and modes. Its collaborative nature is among its greatest challenges. Reaching agreement regarding motivation for change, indicators of goal attainment, target conditions, and value-added outcomes requires deep discussion, often at an unprecedented level of intensity and revelation.

The University of Missouri, for example, uses the Balanced Scorecard approach to address the multiple dimensions of assessment and to measure performance and progress against its strategic plan (see www.system.missouri.edu/urel/SP2001.html). Other universities, such as the California State University at Monterey Bay (csumb.edu/academic/ulr) and Brigham Young (www.byu.edu/academy), have made a significant commitment to student or learning outcomes assessment. The University of Maryland is identifying a set of outcome measures for each of the goals set forth in its strategic plan, and IT staff members are collaborating with those responsible for assessment in other functional areas to coordinate and integrate their efforts (www.oit.umd.edu/ITforUM/2001/Spring/plan).

It is especially difficult to command the required sustained engagement of faculty in any such transformative assessment program. Confronted with this reality, administrators and faculty tend to revert to the superficiality that allows them to retreat to traditional political and intellectual relationships with which everyone is familiar and comfortable.

An example that runs counter to this assertion is the Student Learning Objectives (SLO) project at the University of Washington (see depts.washington.edu/grading/slo/SLO-Home.htm). According to Friedman (2003), associate provost for academic planning, SLO is an effort "to identify learning objectives for its undergraduate learning experiences across the entire University" and to align and integrate those objectives at the program level. Faculty members are identifying student learning objective metrics at the course level, and the university is using e-portfolios to enable students to identify their own learning objectives. Friedman goes on to say that "educational transformation has been inhibited by the suite of metrics available to keep track of student progress. Credits have served as the critical measure of progress; requirements about how many of which kind serve as the rules. The SLO initiative offers an additional set of metrics, one which is designed to enable, rather than restrict, the transformation agenda."

Acknowledging the political and cultural realities of assessment in higher education, Dziuban and Moskal (2002) emphasize that assessment must be both quantitative and qualitative, and it must serve to further both knowledge about learning outcomes, for example, and overall institutional goals (for example, whether there was a positive impact on the institution, as well as on the student).[2] Their admonition demonstrates a practical awareness of the politics of assessment, which is a significant factor in higher education.

Realistically, assessment in higher education must take into account academic culture, campus politics, and, increasingly, expectations about outcomes by multiple constituencies. Dziuban and Moskal play an important role in the assessment efforts used by the

University of Central Florida (UCF) to monitor and inform its transformation process. UCF president John Hitt states that goals must be simple enough to be remembered and measured (Hitt and Hartman, 2002). This is especially important in attaining and sustaining alignment among the many directional thrusts of a complex university.

Similarly, Graves argues that higher education needs to measure and communicate its value to multiple external constituencies. Much as we would like to believe that "one size fits all" and that one set of values and customs should prevail, "higher education leaders . . . need to help their internal constituencies understand the difference between education as a societal good and education as a private good, the forces that are bringing that distinction to the fore, and the need to pursue strategies that depend on the nature of the goals that the strategies are intended to achieve" (Graves, 2002, p. 42).

Assessment in higher education needs to move rapidly from being overly simplistic, business oriented, and quantitative to becoming exceedingly complex to take into consideration the unique aspects of the institution and the expectations of that institution's many constituencies, for example, students, faculty, parents, alumni, boards, politicians, and funding agencies to name a few. The enabling role that IT plays in meeting their varied expectations makes IT assessment particularly sensitive, important, and challenging.

Conclusion

Each of the three methodologies discussed in the first section of this chapter has its place within the IT assessment framework on college and university campuses, but such assessment needs more than just input measures, satisfaction surveys, and self-assessment. We need to look at input measures and satisfaction as part of a broader, multidimensional approach, and we need to focus on real institutional outcomes.

Higher education has yet to step up to the challenge of measuring the outcomes of its teaching, learning, and research. Researchers can measure the movement of subatomic particles and the radiation and other effects of nebulae that have never been seen. However, when it comes to measuring and assessing the impact and effectiveness of teaching, learning, and research on our own campuses, we all too often hear that such an effort is too difficult. Whether because we have not yet learned how to do this effectively or have merely avoided it is irrelevant. Society is becoming increasingly intolerant of such responses.

For assessment to be valid and for it to communicate accurately and effectively to multiple constituencies, it must be multidimensional and collaborative; it must be supported by a cadre of research professionals who conduct their work with a savvy blend of methodological expertise and practical sensitivity to the cultural and political realities of higher education; and it must engage and earn the commitment of the highest levels of the institution's academic and administrative leadership.

Transformative assessment seems the most promising path to achieve this more encompassing approach that is so desperately needed. Without such efforts, evaluating IT in isolation is likely to result in futile and frustrating results that will impede the kinds of change that higher education must effect in the information age.

Notes

1. The READY Tool (www.educause.edu/ready) is a sophisticated assessment and decision tool for engaging leadership in the dialogue regarding distributed learning and for assessing an institution of higher education's stage of readiness for distributed learning, as well as a means of ensuring that decision makers ask, and answer, the right questions, and participate collectively and appropriately in such decisions.

2. Chuck Dziuban and Patsy Moskal's Transformative Assessment Project (TAP) Online Workshop, held April 22, 2002, was a

joint project of the National Learning Infrastructure Initiative, the Coalition for Networked Information, and the Flashlight Project. The objective of TAP is to identify the significant measures of progress and the rubrics of a framework for transformative assessment. The results will be published separately.

References

Dziuban, C., and Moskal, P. On-line presentation, Transformative Assessment Project Online Workshop, Apr. 22, 2002. [www.educause.edu/nlii/keythemes/transformative.asp].

Friedman, D. "Student Learning Objectives (SLO) and the Transformation of the Learning Experience." Presentation, National Learning Infrastructure Initiative annual meeting, New Orleans, Jan. 2003.

Graves, W. H. "An Updated Perspective on the NLII Agenda." *EDUCAUSE Review*, 2002, 37(4), 42. [www.educause.edu/ir/library/pdf/erm0242.pdf].

Green, K. C. *Campus Computing 2001: The Twelfth National Survey of Computing and Information Technology in American Higher Education.* Encino, Calif.: Campus Computing Project, 2001.

Harris, K., Grey, M., and Rozwell, C. *Changing the View of ROI to VOI— Value on Investment.* SPA-14-7250. Stamford, Conn.: Gartner Research, Nov. 14, 2001.

HEIRAlliance Evaluation Guidelines for Institutional Information Resources. Boulder, Colo.: CAUSE, 1995. [www.educause.edu/collab/heirapapers/hei2000.html#docs].

Hitt, J., and Hartman, J. "Distributed Learning: New Challenges and Opportunities for Institutional Leadership." *Distributed Education: Challenges, Choices, and a New Environment*, no. 3. Washington, D.C.: American Council on Education and EDUCAUSE, 2002.

Knox, M. *Information Infrastructure Investment: Communicating the Need to Senior Management.* Stamford, Conn.: Gartner Research, 2002.

New Business Architecture Planning Group. *UC2010: A New Business Architecture for the University of California.* Oakland: University of California, 2001. [http://uc2010.ucsd.edu].

Rhodes, F. *The Creation of the Future: The Role of the American University.* Ithaca, N.Y.: Cornell University Press, 2001.

Smallen, D., and Leach, K. "Seven Benchmarks for Information Technology Investments." *EDUCAUSE Quarterly*, 2002, 25(3), 22–27. [www.educause.edu/ir/library/pdf/eqm0234.pdf].

Warlick, C. *Directory of Computing Facilities in Higher Education*. Austin: University of Texas, 1971–1990.

Index